Faith Seeking
UNDERSTANDING

Faith Seeking
UNDERSTANDING

Approaching
God
Through Science

JOHN M. SHACKLEFORD

Paulist Press
New York/Mahwah, NJ

Library of Congress Cataloging-in-Publication Data

Shackleford, John M.
    Faith seeking understanding : approaching God through science / John M. Shackleford.
        p. cm.
    Includes bibliographical references.
    ISBN 978-0-8091-4451-8 (alk. paper)
    1. Religion and science. 2. Creation. 3. God—Proof, Cosmological. I. Title.
    BL240.3.S49 2007
    261.5'5—dc22

                                                                    2007013293

Published by Paulist Press
997 Macarthur Boulevard
Mahwah, New Jersey 07430

www.paulistpress.com

Printed and bound in the
United States of America

CONTENTS

Dedication

To my three Jeanne Maries
Mother, Daughter, Granddaughter

and to
Granddaughter Meg
Daughter, Petty
Sister-in-law, Petty

PREFACE

For more than thirty years, I taught the biomedical sciences in two medical schools and a dental school. For all that time, I was confined to a wheelchair, which may have given me a small nudge in the direction of theology. Suffering does tend to make us think more often of ultimate questions. Nevertheless, I did not think a great deal about God because I was too busy publishing papers, sending off grant applications for more research dollars, and teaching my classes.

When I retired in 1990, circumstances began to change for me. I was getting older, for one thing, and had recently been forced to undergo bypass surgery on some plaque-filled coronary arteries. It was then that some of the thoughts that had been haunting me over the years blossomed. I returned to the classroom, this time as a student, not a teacher; this time in a theology course, not science. Two and a half years later I received a master's degree in theology, and again began to do some teaching, this time in theology.

The buildings on the campus of the Jesuit college where I attended these classes were old and not very wheelchair accessible. I ascended to third-floor classes in a small, cagelike conveyance. It was an elevator, actually, but a very small one that shook and rattled all the way from the basement to the third floor of the building. I tended to say a few prayers each time I got on the thing, ending with a prayer of thanksgiving after it had carried me safely to my destination.

One night I dreamed I was going up on that rattling, shaking cage of an elevator. In the dream I was surprised when the engine kept on running, taking me past the third floor and up into the attic of that ancient Jesuit building. When I arrived in the attic, I was again surprised. A little old man who apparently had been living up there in the rafters greeted me. He was overjoyed to see me. He told me he had been living in that attic for such a long, long time, and was terribly lonely. He was delighted to see me because now he had somebody to talk with, to engage in conversation. He even hugged me.

Now, this was the kind of dream that one awakens from with a warmth of good feelings. Naturally I wondered what it might suggest, or if it had any meaning at all. I thought about that dream for a long time, wondering about a possible interpretation. I finally concluded that it did, indeed, have a meaning for me. My conclusions are as follows:

That was me, of course, going up on the elevator, passing the third floor, and arriving in the attic of the old building. But the little man living in the rafters was also me (or another part of me). The part of me going up in the elevator was the scientist, the investigator, the aspect of my humanity grounded in the material world—the ambitious, self-centered me. The little man who lived in the attic represented the spiritual side, the aspect of my humanity I had too-long neglected. But going up to the attic, I now had the chance for union between these two aspects of my personality, a possibility of becoming more complete, more authentically human.

The dream was telling me this good news.

INTRODUCTION

Given the loving, personal God of the Judeo-Christian tradition, it seems one must regard science as a gift from the Creator, rather than an intrinsic enemy of the same creative act. We would not exist were it not for the laws of physics and the unique biochemical makeup of the human body. Indeed, living organisms of any sort are marvels of natural engineering. We are a work in progress, from the day we emerge from our mother's womb until our last day on earth. And just as we humans are a work in progress, so is the universe as a whole. Humankind must learn to cooperate in this great strategy of God.

A tree falling in a lifeless wilderness makes no noise because some kind of nervous system is needed to translate the pressure waves into sound. God does not want to be the creator of a sterile universe. This is an answer to the "why" of the so-called *anthropic principle* (humanity reflecting on it origins). In a manner of speaking we can "hear" the big bang and "see" the expanding universe through the eyes and ears of science. The Creator made the universe large enough for exploding nova to occur, spilling the newly formed, heavier elements— those necessary for life—into the cosmic continuum. Through this ordered process came all the chemicals needed to make the first living beings. Finally, God's magnificent creation came under the scrutiny of the pinnacle of biological evolution, the human being. God does not want to be a tree falling in a lifeless wilderness.

Of course, one can accept the biophysical marvels of living things and yet reject the notion that human beings should seek to understand them. It is amazing to see how some of us compartmentalize science and, separately, religion. The spiritual nature of humankind, they would say, has nothing to do with the sciences or any of its manifestations. Further, these opponents of science would contend, it is the scientific world that drags down one's spiritual aspi-

1

rations. Such individuals certainly would not regard scientific curiosity as a gift from God.

This book argues that intellectual pursuits (especially those of science) should be an inherent part of any spiritual endeavor. This idea is actually an ancient one. St. Anselm (1037–1109) advises us that faith and the intellect are partners in understanding the reality in which we live. He wrote

> As the right order requires us to believe the deep things of Christian faith before we undertake to discuss them by reason; so to my mind it appears a neglect if, after we are established in the faith, we do not seek to understand what we believe. *Cur Deus Homo* (I, c.2)

Thus science is also a theological endeavor, at least for the faithful. In seeking God through the intellect, I am not advising that one should abandon faith in order to do so, even if such a purposeful divorce were possible. Rather, the idea of the present work is to explore the likelihood of an invisible God who becomes knowable (less hidden) through science. One might ask, "Is a creator God a *reasonable* intellectual pursuit?" If so, where does scientific curiosity fit in with the concept of salvation, a belief in life after death, and so on? Where is humanity heading, and what role does science play in the whole scheme of human existence?

If there is a personal God, the laws of physics are the basic stuff of his creation. Having made the laws of nature, does God then sustain them, or is he a "clockmaker" God, who sets things in motion, winds up the clock as it were, then sits back and watches it tick away, not caring about any personal involvement? Many believe in such an impersonal force. Stephen Hawking, the famous theoretical physicist, said as much as a guest on the *Larry King Live* show.

Assuming that a loving God is present to us in history, although hidden, why bother to make such a weak and vulnerable creature as the human being? The apostle Paul has an answer for this very question. It is because "God's power is made perfect in weakness" (2 Cor 12:9). God has the power to save us, but that power, if unused, will never be complete (or perfect). The Greek word Paul uses here (*teleitai*) can be translated as either "perfect" or "complete." There is

2

no corresponding answer for the atheistic scenario. Intellectually, therefore, the creation of human beings makes no sense in the absence of a personal God.

In looking for clues to the eternal through science, we may ask ourselves the perennial question, "Why is there something rather than nothing?" In scientific terms, why was there a big bang, or living beings, or an evolutionary process leading to higher forms of life? Is science able to answer these questions in any definitive way? Certainly not. Can science help us to understand the creative process going on in an earthly context, as well as in ourselves? Certainly it can. Why is it important to seek out the meaning of earthly or astronomical things? How can this help us to believe in a personal God, perhaps more fervently? How, indeed, is science related to the spiritual life of each individual, as well as of the human race as a whole? Do we have science just to make us more comfortable, or, through its abuse, to destroy all living things?

As always, we humans have more questions than answers. This is how it should be. During the eighteenth-century Enlightenment, some believed there were no mysteries in the universe, only questions waiting to be answered by science. But even now, in the third millennium CE, the number of questions for science to answer continue to grow. It seems obvious that we will always have mysteries with us, both scientific and theological ones. The "god" of science is just as mysterious as is the personal God of Christians, Jews, and Muslims. What are we looking for, then, to make the Creator God more open to us through science?

It will not help in our quest to discover more subatomic particles, or more supernovas, or distant galaxies, although these discoveries do have meaning beyond the raw data itself. Even Stephen Hawking has used the "mind of God" metaphor to explain his work in lay terms. It may turn out that there are multiple big bangs occurring, and parallel universes more numerous than all the stars in the galaxies. Perhaps there are dimensions of space-time undreamed of, at least mathematically, but how would such phenomena do more than demonstrate the immensity of creation?

In seeking God through science, I believe, we should look for patterns, ones that are meaningful, ones that tell us more than the scientific data itself. We may have to look at these patterns through the *eyes of faith* to draw conclusions from them. We should never abandon the faith perspective in our search. From the faith perspective, science is a tool to pry open the human mystery. In this endeavor, it matters little how many galaxies there are, or how many parallel universes might exist. One universe will be quite enough to study its patterns. Patterns, as I hope to show, give life to the raw data of science. Like the human body, patterns provide science with a wholeness that is greater than its parts. Thus an atom becomes more than its particles and energy fields. A molecule becomes more than its component atoms. A living cell becomes more than its DNA, subcellular particles, and macromolecules. The face of creation is so much greater than its surface features.

The approach here is much simpler than one might guess. I am not speaking of complexities involving thermodynamics or entropy. The role of these physical laws are important, although not crucial to the argument here. The patterns of creation should be understandable by the average person who reads and has an interest in standing back and looking at the larger picture. From this wider perspective the patterns are *anagogic;* that is, they point to some aspect of reality that transcends the subject being discussed or measured. Such anagogical patterns, as important as they are to one's view of reality, will not convince the intractable atheist, of course. There will always be those among us who insist upon their views, regardless of how limited or narrow they might be. To those individuals, science has a different meaning and purpose as contrasted with those of us who believe in a reality beyond material existence. Indeed, these two perceptions may be viewed as two separate realities.

I think of every human being as a work of art, a beautiful composition. As such, we are a work in progress. All of us have a song to sing and a story to tell. Some tell their story in the quietness of the soul, by acting as living examples for others to follow. Then, there are those of us who are compelled by the beauty of the human composition to sing the song and tell the story ourselves. We may tell it over and over again, as long as there is anyone to listen, because God's creation is, indeed, something to sing of and tell about. This book is dedicated to the magnificent symphony of creation and to the beautiful creatures that inhabit it. There is no doubt in my mind that there is a spiritual message in the material universe that begs to be uncovered. To paraphrase the words of the prophet Isaiah in 52:7, How beautiful upon the mountains are the feet [of science] that bring glad tidings [of the God of creation]. Indeed, the footprints of science hint at the path we should follow in seeking out the majestic beauty of God's creation.

REASON AND THE REASONABLE

This may well be called the age of criticism, a criticism from which nothing need hope to escape. When religion seeks to shelter itself behind its sanctity, and law behind its majesty, they justly awaken suspicion against themselves, and lose all claim to the sincere respect which reason yields only to that which has been able to bear the test of its free and open scrutiny.

—Immanuel Kant, *Critique of Pure Reason*

To understand where humanity stands regarding its appreciation of reality, especially in the sciences, we must understand the great strides made during the post-Enlightenment critical age, in which Kant played a seminal, if not indispensable, role. Since the great debates of the eighteenth century, philosophy has grown and matured. It has plumbed its depths. It has deciphered the code for its limits, although it has not fully defined them. Likewise, faith has traveled the same road in coming to terms with itself. It understands its bailiwick more than ever, elevated as it is to its true position in the flow of human essence by such luminaries as Immanuel Kant and Søren Kierkegaard.

CRITICAL THINKERS OF THE
POST-ENLIGHTENMENT

In the late-eighteenth to the nineteenth century, individuals such as Kant and Kierkegaard turned the philosophical world upside down to an even greater extent than Descartes' philosophy of universal doubt. For those in love with the status quo, these were particularly jolting times in which to live: the very foundations of humankind's ability to solve any kind of ultimate question came under attack. These great thinkers helped to illuminate some of the problems facing science and religion. While critical thinking may represent the apparent seeds of division between religion and science, it is not the threat to religion it was once thought to be. The problem, rather, is a certain mind-set, a habit of thinking, a hangover from a past age that continues to frustrate our resolve to conquer prejudice with clear thinking. As long as one is fixed into this mind-set, there is a failure to see the ultimately *constructive* nature of the dialectic between science and religion. Indeed, if one bothers to look closely, there can be seen here a trend that represents the seeds of unification. It may be necessary to sift through some of the great moments of philosophical debate to find this unifying principle. Nevertheless, I believe it can be identified as the *invincible strategy of God.*

Politically, the late-eighteenth century witnessed the American and French revolutions, with their insistence on fundamental human rights and the limitation of governmental authority. This new outlook arose from the proposition that government derives from the consent of the governed, which many began to realize was a fundamental human right.

Technologically, many marvelous new inventions brought delight and convenience to the larger populations. The steamboat, the steam locomotive, the telegraph, the telephone, and the phonograph revolutionized travel and communication. Advances in electricity, photography, medicine, surgery; the overall growth of industry—all these things changed lives drastically for millions. Soon these times began to be known as the *Age of Progress.*

In philosophy, radical doubt had been very much the order of the day from Descartes on. Then, in the century of the *Enlightenment,* many of the philosophical precepts of the Renaissance would be questioned. Religious scholarship, while not caving in before its critics, had to admit that, even from its own perspective, the attacks were partially valid. On the whole, these admissions have been healthy for religion and its practices.

Immanuel Kant (1724–1804)

Kant's entire well-ordered life, with the exception of a negligible period, was spent in the East Prussian city of Königsberg. Beginning as a theology student, he rose to full professor of philosophy, becoming one of the greatest philosophers of all times. He developed what he considered a philosophical revolution parallel in significance to that of Copernicus in astronomy. Kant maintained that we can never know reality-in-itself *(noumenon)* with certitude, but only the thing as it presents itself to the intellect *(phenomenon)*. Indeed, he maintained that true knowledge can never go beyond experience. We can know for sure, therefore, only colors, sounds, appearances, and the like. Thus, Kant, in his *Critique of Pure Reason,* demonstrated that the human intellect cannot conclude existence from essence, and thus opposed the ontological proof for the existence of God put forth by Anselm; nor can existence be concluded from causality per Aristotle and Thomas Aquinas (Wahl, *A Short History of Existentialism,* 8).

In rejecting the cognitive claims of metaphysics and theology, Kant did not propose to banish them from the human scene as meaningless forms of self-indulgence, as some others of this period would do. To the contrary, the religious and moral dimensions of the human personality were to be preserved and given their own specific rationale distinct from scientific reason. The sources of validity of these spheres were to be the *moral will* and *faith,* which provide a different set of data from those of scientific investigations and reasoning. In this instance, we pass from a critique of reason, as reason's own interrogation of itself, to a critique from a point of view outside of reason. Accordingly, the way was thrown open for philosophers to take the leap beyond reason in order to see how reason might appear from the outside (Barrett, *Philosophy in the Twentieth Century,* vol. 3, 128).

Kant, therefore, had no desire to throw out the baby with the bathwater by abolishing the realms of moral will and faith. To satisfy these demands of human nature, he wrote the *Critique of Practical Reason,* in which he acknowledged that, although science could never deal with these ultimate things, humans, in their ethical striving, are called upon to live as if they had immortal souls, and as if there were a God who providentially guided the destinies of the world. In our "inner conscience," Kant believed, we touch a reality more absolute than anything in science.

Georg Wilhelm Friedrich Hegel (1770–1831)

It is this gentleman that we can thank for introducing the idea of an ongoing *dialectic* in society and in history. What is not appreciated by many is the healthy nature of the dialectic, although it has taken us through some very perilous and painful times, especially in our recent history. Hegel asserted that reality should be seen as changing, tumultuous, and filled with conflict, a process he called *Absolute Spirit*. Absolute Spirit moves through history, not abstractly, but deeply involved in exchange and turmoil. This spirit, or *Geist,* becomes a theme in describing a particular civilization's habitual thinking; that is, the spirit of the times, or *Zeitgeist*. People can become more or less trapped in their own outlook until something comes along to break the spell. Hegel's threefold dialectic—*thesis, antithesis, and synthesis*—as proposed in his important work *The Philosophy of History,* continues to have a lasting influence on philosophers of history. Numerous great thinkers in England, America, Italy, and France have testified that they owed to Hegel, not only an increased knowledge, but the fundamental principles of their own thinking as well (Runes, *Treasury of Philosophy*, 474).

Hegel's philosophy has often been regarded as abstract speculation with no practical worth. Yet, soon after his death, it became evident that his works could offer an ideological basis to political parties that are radically opposed to each other. Marx and, after him, Lenin adapted the Hegelian view to give reasons for the doctrine of the proletariat. By contrast, however, even staunch defenders of liberalism and democracy have appealed to Hegel's philosophy of history.

A simplified analogy of the Hegelian dialectic would be the process between the two major political parties in the United States. Suppose, as an example, the Democrats propose some new and important legislation that the Republicans object to vigorously on grounds that it contains too much "pork." Each side gives a little until Congress comes up with a compromise bill suitable to both parties, yet different from what either side would have wanted, had there been no opposition. The original Democrat version represents the *thesis,* the opposing Republican version represents the *antithesis,* and the final, compromise bill represents the *synthesis*. If the new bill later comes up for modification, it then becomes a new *thesis*. Hegel, of course, envisaged a much broader and more spiritually profound context for his dialectic, but the principle is, nevertheless, similar to this political analogy.

In applying the Hegelian dialectic to explain the conflict between science and religion, I am painting the historical stage in broad strokes. There is nothing we do or say, conversationally or formally, trivial or profound, that does not in some measure relate to religion and science. Ultimately, of course, these two disciplines relate to one all-encompassing reality, although we tend to think of them as warring parties (because they often are). Kings' armies, peasant revolts, or mind-numbing excesses of the flesh all relate to the grand picture of history, the stage upon which the dialectic between science and religion is being played out. Most see the problem as one in which somebody wins and somebody loses: religion must die when science triumphs, or science must fade into the background while religion dominates.

But the dialectic, as I am attempting to demonstrate, has no loser. Everyone is a winner. It is the process that leads us to maturity, not at this very moment, but certainly in the future. What is going on between science and religion is ultimately healthy. The only unhealthy thing about the process is the lack of understanding of how the dialectic works to our eventual benefit, how it fits into the grand strategy of God for the uplifting of humankind. It is within this milieu of misunderstanding that we will eventually expose the "demons" that separate science and religion. We are not allowing God to do for us what is in our best interest. Indeed, it boils down to a lack of vision on the part of science, and a lack of faith on the part of religion. As one can see from what follows, some people, like Marx greatly misinterpreted the dialectic and tried to make a tool of it with which to justify all sorts of crimes against humanity.

Karl Marx (1818–1903)

A German, Marx began his academic career in the study of law, but changed to philosophy, taking a PhD degree at the University of Jena in 1841. He was very much influenced by Hegel's system, but even more so by that of Ludwig Feuerbach (1804–72). Feuerbach was a materialist who believed humankind evolved the idea of God to rec-

11

oncile all the contradictions of life. Marx joined the Communist League in 1847. The following year he wrote, with Friedrich Engels, the *Communist Manifesto.* Marx's principal work, *Das Kapital,* which first appeared in 1867, developed his views on modern economic life.

Building upon the views of Hegel and Feuerbach, Marx perceived reality as motion, struggle, and turmoil; to him the universe was godless, without creator or general intelligence. In short, Marx turned Hegel's threefold dialectic idealism to one of dialectic materialism.

Marx viewed humanity, like everything else in the universe, as governed by the cosmic law of struggling material in motion. Marx can be faulted for discounting the importance of family, character, faith, and so on, that have been seen as primary social-identity factors. On the other hand, his prevailing insight was that individuals quickly become locked into grinding, life-sapping jobs with no prospect for education, advancement, or human aspirations.

Marx therefore called on the workers of the world to unite. He was a materialist and a believer in great possibilities for humankind. Humanity, believed Marx, can advance to a better relationship living in a classless and stateless society. Marx's diagnosis of troubled humanity was this: alienation. Men and women are not truly at home in the world. They are aliens. Marx could see no remedy for this condition within the framework of the unchecked capitalism of mid-nineteenth-century Europe and America. His remedy, therefore, was nothing short of violent revolution. He sought to dethrone the *haves* by the *have-nots,* while seizing the means of production along with abolishing private property.

As the system developed in practice, the conclusion was reached that the great masses of people were so oppressed that they didn't know what was best for themselves. An elite cadre—the (Communist) Party—needed to take up the banner and lead the people *even if they were unwilling.* The undemocratic means would be justified by the great end of a transformed humanity. The ends, therefore, justify the means.

Marx saw the world in terms of a conflict between the economically powerful and the economically powerless. From that point of view, he considered religion as a major power working to maintain an unjust status quo. This was accomplished by turning the minds of its adherents toward an afterlife of supposed redress of injustices. But the path to that heavenly utopia was based on passive acceptance of things as they exist in the present. Thus he formulated his famous claim that religion was the "sigh of the oppressed creature" and the "opium of the people." The reaction of religious scholars to Marx takes two forms:

1. They agree that religion has, in fact, often been used as a retrogressive force in society. But this occurrence does not negate the ultimate claims of religion or its value to society. A good thing can be used badly.
2. They point out that as workers gain more affluence, their religious needs do not wither, but rather can be said to increase. Relieved from the sheer struggle for survival and basic needs, workers begin to seek out a meaning for the human enterprise in a more fundamental sense.

THE EXISTENTIALISTS

We next come to the movement in history called *existentialism*, which reached great prominence in the twentieth century. It is of interest not because it was against religion or antiscience. It was neither. In fact, it became an umbrella philosophy for all sorts of people, scientist and nonscientist, atheist and theist, Protestant and Roman Catholic, Jew and Gentile. Existentialism is worth examining, then, simply because it represents the end of a long history of dialectic in the guise of philosophical dispute. For many it became a meeting place in which different viewpoints could find common expression. It is therefore a very *ecumenical* philosophy, if one can think of any philosophy as such. Existentialism is important because we see in it the seeds of convergence, a trend that yields the all-important fruits of patience and perseverance on the historical stage of humankind. Upon this stage, convergence is a step toward unity, a moment of resonance for humankind with God. In fact, the principal difference among existentialists is their religious stance—whether they are theists or nontheists.

13

The roots of existentialism have been traced to such early thinkers as Augustine and Thomas Aquinas. Immanuel Kant, mentioned earlier as a shaper of philosophical precepts, can be thought of as preparing the ground for existentialist philosophy. Writing at the end of the great century of rationalism, Kant showed in his *Critique of Pure Reason* that the transcendent ideals of our traditional Christian civilization—God, the human soul and its possible immortality, the freedom of each person as a spiritual being—could not be known by human reason. He argued in his *Critique of Practical Reason* that, although science could never deal with ultimate things, humankind in the seriousness of its ethical striving is called upon to live as if each person has an immortal soul, and as if there were a God who providently guides the destinies of the world. Kant held that in our *inner conscience* we touch a reality more absolute than anything in science. The human, or existential, import of Kant's philosophy comes to this: what Kant the man lived by as an ethical and spiritual person, Kant the scientific thinker could not even bring into thought.

The idealist philosophers believed Kant had dug a chasm between two parts of the human personality. The chasm, however, was not of Kant's doing because it already existed, had always existed. Kant simply demonstrated that, although reason could not *fill* the breach, it might *bridge* it. It was left to others as to how this might be done.

Søren Kierkegaard (1813–55)

Enter existentialism. The moment was perfectly timed in this great human drama of Western thought. The situation was ripe for a philosophical revolt, which came in the persons of Søren Kierkegaard and Friedrich Nietzsche, the two individuals who are generally accepted as the founding fathers of existential philosophy. Kierkegaard put an end to the totalitarian claims for reason made by philosophers (Dupre, *Kierkegaard as Theologian*). If religion could be reduced to reason, said Kierkegaard, there would be no need for religion, least of all a religion like Christianity whose central belief in a God-man is altogether paradoxical to reason.

As a believing Christian, Kierkegaard insisted on the necessity of faith as a vital act beyond reason. The existence of the individual

Christian, as he brought out, could never be enclosed in any system. First of all, the existent individual is one who is in an infinite relationship with and has an infinite interest in one's self and destiny. Second, the existent individual always feels oneself to be in a state of *becoming,* always with a task before one. Applying this idea to Christianity, Kierkegaard believed that one is not a Christian, one always *becomes* a Christian—it is a matter of sustained effort. Kierkegaard gives a more urgent and powerful expression to the Kantian view that each of us, as individuals, touch reality inwardly in our moments of serious moral decision rather than in the detached speculations of reason. Kierkegaard says of Kant's values, however, that they cannot be kept alive by reflection on the "postulates of practical reason"; in the end, Kant's values can be kept alive only by the energy of faith.

Friedrich Nietzsche (1844–1900)

In his book *The Shattered Lantern,* Ronald Rolheiser takes up Nietzsche's theme—"God is dead," and "we are his murderers"—and tries to analyze why modern faith in God is so culturally shaken. It is an insightful book in that it identifies some of the societal obstacles one must overcome to regain the closeness to God we once felt as a people. The book does not touch on the relationship of science and religion, as does the present work, and therefore misses an important element affecting our faith in the twentieth century. Much of the agnosticism and narcissism Rolheiser speaks of has its roots in the old conflict between science and religion. This conflict, however, in spite of some of the vitriol that springs from the perceived rivalry between the two sides, is a good and healthy dialogue. It is part of God's overall strategy for human growth and maturity, even for our salvation. We cannot rid ourselves of this conflict by pretending it is not there.

Nietzsche is the author of *Thus Spake Zarathustra,* a fable that developed his ideas and dreams of a race of "supermen." Some believe the work influenced Adolf Hitler to attempt ethnic cleansing on a massive scale to rid Germany of its Jewish population. Nietzsche, in spite of his atheism, would have been appalled to hear that some have associated his philosophy with the likes of Hitler.

15

Nietzsche starts from the same historical insight as Kierkegaard, but attacks Kant from the "opposite" direction. To Nietzsche, the blind old prejudice of Kant's religious precepts should be thrown on the dust heaps of history. Is not Christianity already dead, or dying, although some still give it lip service? But Nietzsche did not stop here, for he speculated on the time when God is at last dead for humankind, when the last gleam of light is extinguished, when at last humanity knows it is alone in the world in the impenetrable darkness of the universe. Only then would humankind take responsibility for its actions, making possible a new era of human progress. The disappearance of religion would be the greatest challenge in human history, for humanity would then be fully and dreadfully responsible *to itself* and *for itself*. So Nietzsche's answer to the widening chasm between science and religion was simply to do away with God (and religion, too). There can be no chasm, no breach, if there is nothing on the other side to define it.

Jean-Paul Sartre (1905–80)

A French existentialist, Sartre wrote the difficult treatise *Being and Nothingness,* but he is better known for his novel *Nausea* and the play *No Exit.* Sartre remained a Marxist all his adult life. In Sartre's universe, like that of Nietzsche, there is no God over destiny and purpose. He presumes the absence of God in the world as a settled cultural fact. The universe, therefore, has no meaning except that with which human freedom invests it. Man is *condemned to freedom.* We simply exist, not having been created or evolved for any purpose. We are here and we have to decide what to make of it all. Life, for many at least, is a useless passion. Each individual, in freedom, chooses the meaning of his or her own particular life, and this freedom terrifies us.

Psychologists have commented on this same freedom/flight phenomenon. Fear of genuine responsibility is never far below the human surface, and that fear may account as much for authoritarianism and totalitarianism in the world as perhaps power-mongers seeking personal might. It is not so much the strength of the individual "taker of freedom" that is the cause of society's ills, say these psychologists, as it is the willingness of so many to give it up. Thus, humanity-at-large flees from freedom and gives itself over in servitude to social, political, and religious systems that are all too willing to take advantage of this human dilemma. Religious thinkers may agree with Sartre on the point that faith or a life-stance that is merely "inherited" or uncritically assimilated can hardly be called *authentic faith*. One must choose something to believe. Otherwise we simply occupy space. Lack of commitment to a belief system is a commitment to nothing, to biological functions and time tables, to a life as one of the living dead.

Sartre is not very strong on a practical remedy for the human dilemma he sees in his philosophy. If, for example, self-knowledge and self-actualization are primary values, if all things are utterly pointless, then on what basis must one opt for freedom over tyranny, for tenderness over terror?

Gabriel Marcel (1889–1973)

In contrast to Sartre, Marcel takes an existential view of humanity's condition from the Christian perspective in his book *The Ontological Mystery*. The modern person, says Marcel, has lost the sense of what it is to be human; that is, of one's *being*, one's very essence. Generally speaking, if ontological demands (ultimate concerns) worry humankind at all, they are felt only dully, as an obscure impulse. Marcel wonders if a psychoanalytical method, deeper and more discerning than any that has been evolved until now, would not reveal the morbid effects of the repression of this sense, of the ignoring of this ontological need.

The individual, says Marcel, tends to appear both to oneself and to others as an *agglomeration* of functions. As a result of deep historical causes, which can as yet be understood only in part, the person has been led to see more and more the inward assemblage of functions as the definition of human life. The rather horrible expression *time table* perfectly describes human life. So many hours for each function. Sleep, too, is a function that must be discharged so that the other functions may be exercised in turn; the same with pleasure, relaxation, sex, and so on. Marcel agrees with other existentialists in placing emotions, such as anxiety and despair, at the center of human existence. Where he differs, however, is in his determined effort to get at the root of the despair. He explains, therefore, that a world centered on function is liable to despair because in reality this world is empty. It is a world riddled with problems and, on the other hand, a reality determined to allow no room for mystery. In such a world the ontological need is exhausted in proportion to the breaking up of the personality, and the consequent atrophy of the faculty of wonder.

There is a partial response to Marcel's longing for a psychoanalytic solution to humankind's ontological need in the researches of C. G. Jung. Certainly Jung believed he had discovered (uncovered) this *need* in his experience as a clinical psychologist (see chapter 7). Over and over Jung emphasized that he was a scientist, not a philosopher or theologian. His investigations in the field of the human psyche, however, have greatly influenced these other disciplines. One can find in almost any city in the United States with a sizable population a Jungian society. Jung and his dedicated followers, therefore, have done more to link together psychology and religion—in identifying if not quantifying this ontological need of Gabriel Marcel—than any other psychological movement.

COMMON BONDS OF EXISTENTIALISM

One idea that ties all existentialists together is that *existence precedes essence;* that is to say, in agreement with Kant's philosophy, one cannot reach any understanding of essences (the essence, or *being,* of God, human *being,* and so on) through reason alone. This idea is reflected in the title of Jean-Paul Sartre's treatise on existentialism, *Being and Nothingness.* In addition, the existentialists place primal emotions—such as fear, hope, love, anxiety, insecurity—at the center of their reality. Heidegger, a German existentialist, used the word *forlornness* to describe *being-in-the-world* because experience is pervaded with, and gripped by, anxiety.

An awareness of ourselves as *existents* is attainable only by traversing certain experiences, like that of anguish, which put us in the presence of the background of *nothingness* from which *being* erupts. Kierkegaard insisted upon the experience of anguish as a revelation of the possibilities that lie beyond.

Perhaps I should mention here the difference between the ideas of *essence* and *accident* as they apply to *being.* An individual man may

Reason and the Reasonable

have brown hair, work as a salesman, and have a tendency to indigestion if he eats foods that are too spicy. These types or characteristics might be referred to as *accidents* of that person, because he may or may not share any or all of these things with his fellow humans. The aspect that is universally shared, however, is his *being,* his humanness, or, in the Aristotelian sense, his essence. It is that which makes us human rather than a dog or a monkey or an oyster. The characteristics that *all* human beings share in common, therefore, make up the human essence.

Exactly what constitutes that human essence, the essence of God, or the essence of anything, for that matter, is a point of disagreement among philosophers. This is what existentialism is all about, in that its proponents maintain we cannot arrive at essences (human, God, or whatever) from reason alone. But the existentialists go beyond the mere limitations of reason in their view of existence. Individual human beings and their primal emotions, drives, and feelings are at the center of existential concern, not general theories. Thus, the inner *subjective* experience of the individual is more revealing about reality than is the outer *objective* truth of science: meaning and interpretation take precedence over mere facticity. More than any other thing, freedom is the defining human capacity. To be authentic (truly free), individuals must *choose* their own interpretations, meaning, and values in life.

GATHERING THE FORCES OF DIVERSITY

It may seem that all of the diverse elements of human thought, as represented in the various philosophic movements over the centuries, have little to do with human order and consistency, and everything to do with human confusion. The thesis of this book, however, is just the opposite. One can see in these historical events a growing consciousness of ultimate meaning in the universe, an increasing awareness of purposeful existence, instead of what may have seemed before to be a manifestation of eternal chaos. One has to step outside the existential approach to the human situation to see these positive forces. It is essential, therefore, to examine history with the eyes of faith.

Faith Seeking Understanding

One could say that the forces of the universe continue to converge in the marvelous creation of the human mind. All the scattered elements, as Teilhard de Chardin might say, are gathering before our eyes. These sparks come together as a mighty fire in the hearts of God's human creatures. Only in ignoring the sparks does humankind fail to comprehend the fire.

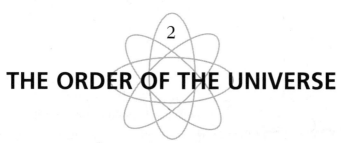

THE ORDER OF THE UNIVERSE

> You must have often wondered why the Enemy [God] does not make more use of His power to be sensibly present to human souls in any degree He chooses and at any moment. But now you see that the Irresistible and the Indisputable are the two weapons which the very nature of His scheme forbids Him to use.
>
> —C. S. Lewis, *The Screwtape Letters*

Why does God just not reveal himself—indisputably—to each person? C. S. Lewis gives a lucid answer to this difficult question in his famous *Screwtape Letters,* in which Screwtape himself (a chief devil) coaches an apprentice devil, Wormwood. There are many sound, theological reasons why God hides himself. This, however, does not mean that our Creator *wants* to remain hidden.

As in ancient times, we continue to be awed by the vastness of the universe. The more we learn of it, the more awesome it becomes. And yet, Julian of Norwich, one of my favorite mystics, conceives of "everything which is made" as almost insignificant in light of the power and majesty of the One who created it. There has always been, and always will be, a close connection between the observation of the incredibly immense cosmos and the sense of a powerful intelligence behind it all. Yet the science of astronomy drifted apart from these close ties with religion, beginning with the Renaissance and continuing into the eighteenth and nineteenth centuries. In modern times, however, the old connections are beginning to reassert themselves with the discovery of the expanding universe and the big bang theory of its origin. Very few reputable astronomers question the big bang moment of creation, in which order came out of chaos, and material existence out of nonexistence. No one, scientist or layperson, dares to attempt a complete explanation of this momentous event, but one can hardly exclude a Supreme Intelligence from the original equation in which time and space began out of nothing. Even if the universe in which we live somehow "bled" into existence from some kind of parallel universe, the question remains the same: "Why is there something rather than nothing?" Most of us associate creation with a Creator, and it is quite natural to point to the vastness of the universe as reason enough to believe in an intelligence behind it all. From this point of view, *all of creation has sacramental character.*

Indeed, in its broadest sense, the word *sacred* includes all of creation. When Christians assemble in churches, or Hindus bathe in the Ganges, or Muslims make pilgrimages to Mecca, these locations are revered, not because of what they are in themselves, but because of what they symbolize—something *beyond* themselves, something mysterious, something which cannot be seen. In this sense everything that represents a hidden reality is sacramental. Any ritual or object, person or place, can be considered sacramental if it is taken to be a symbol of that which is sacred or mysterious in the religious sense. What, therefore, could be more sacramental than creation itself? As Augustine once noted, according to the general definition of *sacramentum,* anything in the world could be considered a sacrament since all of creation is a sign of God (Martos, *Doors to the Sacred,* 12). Of course, Christians now think of "the sacraments" in a more restricted sense of Eucharist, baptism, confirmation, and so on, but these distinctions do not prohibit one from thinking in terms of the broader symbolic associations. It is in this broader sense, therefore, that we now examine the universe as a whole.

ALL THAT IS MADE

And in this he showed me something small, no bigger than a hazelnut, lying in the palm of my hand, and I perceived that it was round as any ball. I looked at it and thought: what can this be? And I was given this general answer: It is everything which is made. I was amazed that it could last, for I thought that it was so little that it could suddenly fall into nothing.   —Julian of Norwich, *Showings*

The Order of the Universe

At its simplest, the physical universe is composed entirely of matter and energy. All things possess these two forms of existence to one degree or another. It can be said that matter and energy are the same thing in two different forms, in that energy can be converted into matter, and vice versa. The energy of the sun, for example, becomes matter, that is, vegetation. The energy of the sun is thus "trapped" in the matter—moss, leaves, wood—until it is again released by burning or decay. Feeling the heat from a burning log is like feeling the heat of the sun all over again, as the energy of the sun, stored in the wood fiber, is released.

A small amount of matter can be converted into a large amount of energy, as shown by Einstein's $E=MC^2$ (where E equals energy, M equals mass, and C equals the speed of light), and has been dreadfully demonstrated in the explosion of a nuclear bomb. The energy released from burning wood is the energy stored up in the chemical bonds of the wood fiber. In this case there is no matter (mass) lost or destroyed. In a nuclear reaction, however, a small amount of mass actually disappears as it is converted to energy.

Everything that can be said about the physical universe builds on this simple principle of the relationship between matter and energy. Our human bodies, for example, contain the atoms of dead stars created billions of years ago, under conditions of incredibly high temperature and pressure, by intrastellar nuclear reactions. To be sure, it is from the dust and debris of such exploding stars that solar systems such as ours, including their planets and all their planetary life, are formed. Boggles the mind, doesn't it?

Everything we experience in life here in the material universe occupies space in the aspect of three dimensions. In addition, there is a fourth dimension, namely, that of time. We all experience the three dimensions of our existence in terms of time—more specifically, linear time. That is to say, we go to the grocery store and buy bread. The one act (of going to the grocery store) comes before the other (buying the bread). We live and experience linear time in every waking moment and would be lost, or go out of our minds, in its absence. Everyone conceives his or her personal history—birth, adolescence, adulthood, old age, death—in terms of time. We may think in the same way about world history. Civilizations are born and die out; languages come and go. Wars, famine, and epidemics make headlines in one generation, while these same events fade from memory in the next. With the passage of time, current news becomes old news, and old news becomes history.

Theologians tell us that God is timeless, that there is no present or future for God. Is this possible? Could we humans possibly think and exist in a timeless universe if, for example, we crossed over from our universe to the divine dimension of God? How would a person so immersed in time adjust to sudden timelessness? Is it necessary that we *become like God* before such a transformation is possible? Are there other dimensions that we will one day understand when we reach a higher plane of existence? Many Christians believe that humanity *is* becoming like God. According to Athanasius, a Greek father of the church, that is why God became human, that is, so that human beings might become like God.

In an interesting book titled *Hyperspace*, Michio Kaku tells of the possible existence of ten dimensions! Using the advanced formulation of *superstring theory*, Kaku describes how three dimensions of space (and one of time) might be extended by six more *spatial* dimensions. One cannot imagine what a fourth spatial dimension would be like, let alone an additional six. Kaku believes that a person living in a fourth spatial dimension would be like a god to us. He or she could walk through walls, even disappear and reappear some distance from the initial point of departure. In other words, from our tri-dimensional perspective, that person in the fourth dimension could *transubstantiate*.

Recent efforts to arrive at a unified theory, the "theory of everything," as discussed in Hawking's book *The Universe in a Nutshell*, expands Kaku's ten dimensions to a possible eleven. These other spatial dimensions are all quite detached from our perspective and have nothing to do with us (as far as we know) except as an abstract mathematical exercise. I find Hawking's imagery of the universe in a nutshell fascinating. Though the phrase is from Shakespeare's *Hamlet*, fourteenth-century mystic Julian of Norwich, quoted earlier, said that God revealed to her "all that is made" and compared it to the hazelnut. Is this pure coincidence? Could Shakespeare have known of the writings of this saintly woman?

Michio Kaku's book is full of speculative thinking on parallel universes, time warps, black holes, wormholes (perhaps connecting parallel universes), and *God-talk*. God-talk (theological discussion) is becoming more and more common in scientific works that deal with the limits of experimental methods. Kaku's book raises theological questions because the existence of any dimensions, beyond the three spatial dimensions familiar to us, cannot be experimentally proved or disproved.

THE ORIGIN OF THE UNIVERSE

The origin of the universe and the origin of life on Earth are such complex events that it is becoming more and more difficult, even for the scientist, to see them as occurring in a godless universe—or at least without some intelligent strategy behind it all. From the religious point of view, it could be simply stated that God made the universe and everything in it. Why go beyond this simple belief? But then, would we really be faithful believers if we simply let it go at that? Did God give us an intellect and a curiosity without some purpose?

Most of us want to know more of how God went about the job of creating. Certainly it is not a process that we humans have any control over, and just because it is one's conviction that God created in a certain way, that does not make it less a creation. It seems incumbent upon us, therefore, to make use of our God-given intellects to explore just how creation began, including the origin of life itself.

Listening as scientists attempt to describe these events, one has to be prepared to stretch the imagination to the limit. At the big bang itself, says Stephen Hawking, the universe is thought to have had "zero size," and to have been infinitely hot. Time began at the instant of the big bang, and as the universe expanded from this primordial beginning, it began to cool. One second after the big bang, the temperature of primal matter fell to about ten thousand million degrees. At this reduced temperature, the universe "cooled" to about the heat of an H-bomb explosion. A hundred seconds or so later, the temperature fell to one thousand million degrees, or the temperature that would allow for the formation of the first atoms of heavy hydrogen (deuterium) and helium.

After that, theorizes Hawking, for the next million years or so, the universe would have continued expanding without much else happening. With the passage of more time, the hydrogen and helium gases would break up into smaller clouds and contract under the force of gravity into the first stars. In this pristine universe the original stars (suns) would continue in their fusion reactions as they converted more atoms of hydrogen into helium, radiating energy as heat and light.

Because of their more rapid nuclear fusion rates, the more massive stars of this primordial universe (much larger than our own sun) used up their hydrogen fuel faster—in as little as a hundred million years. They then began to contract and, as they did, some of the helium was converted into heavier elements such as carbon and oxygen. As contraction of these giant stars continued, their central-most regions collapsed to a very dense state, as in a neutron star or a black hole. A black hole is not a hole at all, of course. It is so named because the gravitational forces are so great that even light cannot escape its pull. During this stellar crisis, as the massive star begins to collapse, the outer regions may be blown off in a gigantic explosion called a supernova. At this point it would outshine all the other stars in the galaxy, while the exploding mass would provide the raw material for the next generation of stars.

The new solar systems, containing second-generation stars, exhibit vast differences from their primitive forebears, since they contain from their outset the heavier atoms of carbon and oxygen, two principal building blocks of life. Indeed, all life on the planet Earth depends on the carbon atom as the basis for organic compounds, including amino acids (the building blocks of proteins), carbohydrates, and fats. This explains the earlier statement that *we humans contain within our bodies the atoms of long-dead stars.* The formation of life, then, depends on these first-generation giant stars for the basic elements out of which all living things are constructed (for more details on this process see Stephen Hawking's *A Brief History of Time*).

Of course, not just time began with the big bang, but all the dimensions and properties of matter that we have been discussing. In other words, space began where before there was nothing in existence to define space. Our Milky Way galaxy is composed of gas, dust, and billions of stars. Each star may be a sun to someone or something, for within each galaxy there are possibly millions of worlds on which the proliferation of living matter, even intelligent beings, may be developing, or has already come into being. As Carl Sagan writes in his book

Cosmos (20), "We live on a mote of dust circling a humdrum star in the remotest corner of an obscure galaxy." We have come a long way from the time of Ptolemy the astronomer (AD 90–168), when people believed that our Earth was at the center of the universe. Sagan estimates that, in all of the universe, there are some *hundred billion galaxies*, each one of these, on average, with a hundred billion stars. In addition there may be at least as many planets as stars, a small percentage of which (statistically speaking) could be Earth-like. But remember, according to the best scientific minds in the field, it all came out of *nothing*. If, then, the entire universe came from nothing (during the one-thousandth-of-a-second event called the big bang), it could just as easily revert back to its original state. Perhaps Julian of Norwich was correct in her amazed assessment of what the Lord had shown her, for in spite of its vastness, all that was created is "so little that it could suddenly fall to nothing."

The big bang—the beginning of the expanding universe and the beginning of time—is variously estimated to have taken place some fifteen to twenty billion years ago. The solar system that we know, however, including our very own planet Earth, is estimated to be close to a mere five billion years old. Having been formed from the remnants of the tremendous explosion of a supernova, our Earth was very hot at first and was not able to support life for many millions of years. Following this incalculable time of a superheated Earth, the planet cooled sufficiently to allow the first pools of liquid water to form. It was in just such a warm mixture of water and other substances, sometimes referred to as a primordial soup, that scientists speculate life began. Once life appeared, then all kinds of possibilities opened up.

Now, poised at the pinnacle of evolution, human beings can "see" the expanding universe and "hear" the big bang. We accomplish this amazing feat through the eyes and ears of science. The hot frying pan, removed from the stove, is sometimes used to explain the second law of thermodynamics to students. As the frying pan cools, the concentrated energy is dispersed into the air with an accompanying increase in entropy. The universe, however, unlike the cooling frying pan, converts some of its energy into chemical bonds, such as oxygen and carbon. This conversion of energy slows down the increase in entropy as larger atoms are formed. Some of the energy of the primordial (big bang) explosion, therefore, adds a new crust to the material universe as the process converts more and more atoms to complex molecules, from which life itself becomes possible. The crust of living organisms could only occur on a vast creative scale, with the formation of enormous amounts of mass. Otherwise the larger stars would never have come into existence, and without such stellar events life could not have occurred. Or as Owen Gingerich writes (*Evidence of Purpose,* 23):

> [H]ad the original energy of the Big Bang explosion been less, the universe would have fallen back onto itself long before there had been time to build the elements required for life and to produce from them intelligent sentient beings. Had the energy been more, it is quite possible that the density would have dropped too swiftly for stars and galaxies to form.

One might add to this remarkable vision the eyes and ears of faith. What the sensibilities of faith bring to the scientific equation is a conclusion that could not be reached in the absence of the physical phenomena. To be sure, one of the reasons scientific tools are placed at our disposal is because we are *expected* to study God's creation, to center its magnificence under our eyes. Had the creative act been on a smaller scale, life would not have occurred, and human beings would not be here to notice it. So "Why is there something rather than nothing?" is joined by another incisive question: "Why is the universe the size it is?" The answer to both is that, as I've said before, God does not want to be a tree falling in a deserted wilderness, a Creator with no creatures to observe his works.

Carbon is the most common element in the galaxy, next to hydrogen, helium, and oxygen. Carbon, one of the heavier elements formed as a result of the enormous pressures of a star about to go nova, is also the basis of all life on Earth. It turns out that the resonance of the carbon atom is one that predisposes it to form from three helium nuclei. Gingerich (*Evidence of Purpose,* 24), tells of his astronomer friend Fred Hoyle, who with Willy Fowler made this discovery "that nothing has shaken his atheism as much as this discovery."

Most writers in the field of science and religion are quick to point out that none of these scientific phenomena can be regarded as proof for the existence of a personal God, or any god at all, for that matter. To me, however, all such discoveries are a form of divine grace because through them God beckons us to see beyond the data to recognize his presence in our lives and in the glorious universe he created. It may be that we have uncovered an *intelligent design*, or at least a pattern of how creation works, leading up to and centering under the eyes of humankind. The amazing aspect of these researches is that these connections (patterns, designs) are being discovered with increasing frequency. In my seventy-five years on this earth, and in my capacity as a scientist, this unfolding of patterns has certainly been evident to me.

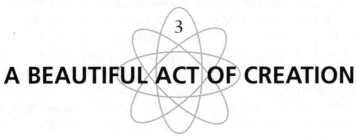

A BEAUTIFUL ACT OF CREATION

Science in its development—and even, as I shall show, mankind in its march—is marking time at this moment, because men's minds are reluctant to recognize that evolution has a precise *orientation* and a privileged *axis*. Weakened by this fundamental doubt, the forces of research are scattered, and there is no determination to build the earth.

—Teilhard de Chardin, *The Phenomenon of Man*

As mentioned in the Introduction, the human species is a work in progress, a beautiful composition, an intricate work of art. We cannot appreciate this reality if we limit the manner in which God creates his biological world. Indeed, biological evolution pours out a certain beauty into the creative act that the faithful should not ignore, even though many Christians, Jews, and Muslims see such ideas as a challenge to their beliefs.

It is perhaps a natural reaction to regard science as a challenge to one's faith. We tend to become comfortable in our beliefs and fearful of any new enterprise that might disturb that peaceful embrace. In my experience, the fear and uncertainty that come with new scientific data are short-lived. In the process of incorporating new ideas into our personal worldview, we invariably grow and mature as authentic human beings. The human work in progress adds a new dimension to one's thinking as we grow stronger in our original beliefs.

Consider the startling makeup of our bodies, composed of atoms originated in long-dead, exploding stars. This new insight, despite the more mundane views we might have entertained previously, grows into a marvelous aspect of creation. The same thing can be said of evolution. Many of us still struggle with this concept because it challenges biblical interpretation, particularly the stories of creation as told in the Book of Genesis. I would venture to say that, for many people, evolution has been, and still is, the greatest challenge ever to belief in a personal God. Here again, in accepting the theory of evolution as a likely manner in which God went about creating the human species, believers find a new dimension of their faith, rather than disparagement of its basic tenets. Of interest here is that the struggle of Christianity over the origin of man began long before Darwin's theory.

One can imagine how the idea of organic evolution, including the presumption that even humankind developed from lower species, must have turned the religious world upside down. It was an outrageous proposition to even think of, said many, much less to proclaim it before an unsuspecting and unprepared public. That was the effect of Darwin's *Origin of Species*, as this 1859 work impacted upon the dignified world of the nineteenth century. Josiah Clark Nott, an American physician and anthropologist, said of Darwin's book, "The man is clearly crazy, but it is a capital dig at the parsons—it stirs up creation & much good comes out [of] such thorough discussion" (Nott to E. George Squier, August 22, 1860; *Squier Papers,* Library of Congress).

BIBLICAL CHRONOLOGY

Before the publication of Darwin's *Origin of Species,* the argument was not over evolution, but the then-current notion of biblical chronology; that is, how the Book of Genesis should be interpreted, if at all, regarding the age of the Earth, the creation of humanity, and so on. The prevailing view, especially among clerics, was that Earth was no more than about six thousand years old. Even Shakespeare agreed with this through Rosalind, the heroine of *As You Like It,* who says: "The poor world is almost six thousand years old." A certain Archbishop Ussher (1581–1656) is famous for his "precise" estimate as to Earth's original formation. Based on study of the Book of Genesis, his chronology said that Earth was created in 4004 BC, on October 26 at nine o'clock in the morning. Ussher's dates were accepted for nearly two centuries, particularly among those who insisted on a literal interpretation of every word of the Bible. Some editions of the King James Version of the Bible included Ussher's chronology. This, then, was the common perception in the world of Josiah Nott and Charles Darwin.

THE AMERICAN SCHOOL OF ANTHROPOLOGY

Throughout his life, Josiah Nott corresponded with many interesting and outstanding men of science. He became embroiled with the leaders of Protestant orthodoxy in a vitriolic argument over the unity of mankind. Nott believed that the races were created separately, as opposed to the biblical idea that all humankind came from Adam and Eve. He and his collaborators, having little idea as to the great age of the planet, based their argument on the Egyptian hieroglyphics depicting the different races as existing side by side even in those ancient times. The heart of the argument between Nott and the "parsons" has been thoroughly reviewed in *The Leopard's Spots,* an outstanding book on the subject by William Stanton. A look at the flavor of the argument, as well as its principal participants, is an essential element in understanding Nott. The arguments are not important in themselves, because Darwinism overtook and replaced the racial outlook of the American School of Anthropology. What is important to show, however, is that the evolutionary theory was not the first challenge to a literal interpretation of the Book of Genesis.

One of Nott's frequent correspondents was Dr. Samuel George Morton, a Philadelphia physician and professor of anatomy. Morton's scientific efforts included his 1834 book, *Synopsis of the Organic Remains of the Cretaceous Group of the United States,* in which he described the fossils collected by Lewis and Clark. Later, in 1839, Morton published his *Crania Americana,* which included descriptions of human skulls collected and sent to Morton from every corner of the United States and "all quarters of the world." Josiah Nott's interest in anthropology (*ethnology,* as it was then called) ran along similar lines to that of Morton. With the publication of *Crania,* there began a long association between the two that lasted until Morton's death in 1851. Following Morton's death, Nott became the undisputed leader of the American School of Anthropology.

In 1844, Morton wrote to Nott and sent a copy of *Crania.* Nott responded that he had read the book with great pleasure, assuring

Morton that its publication would "add not a little" to his reputation. Nott complimented Morton on his conclusion that the races "are distinct," believing that to be the only reasonable interpretation of Morton's data. Nott went on to say that Morton's researches had gone far enough to "blow up all chronologies," although it would not be "very politic" to say so "in these days of Christian intolerance." Nott indicated his admiration for the "code of beautiful morals" as set forth in the Bible, but he hastened to add that the Bible showed "no scientific knowledge beyond the human knowledge of the day" and that "its great ends required no other" (Nott to Morton, October 15, 1849; Historical Society of Pennsylvania).

The war of words between Nott and the "parsons" continued for many years, the hassle becoming more vituperative as time passed. Nott rejoiced, however, that the parsons in Mobile, Alabama, where he practiced medicine, were among his best friends. "I physic every one of them," he told Morton, and "they give me credit for all the Christian virtues…" In October 1849 he was optimistic that the battle had cooled down, saying that he hoped "more liberal views" were beginning to prevail and that "we may be able to arrive at the truth after a while" (ibid.).

But the reprieve did not last long. Dr. Robert W. Gibbes, Nott's old professional associate, remarked in a letter to Morton, "Our friend Nott has brought down upon him the wrath of the clergy in S. C. [South Carolina]." In particular, Gibbes was referring specifically to the wrath of Reverend John Bachman, who was to become Nott's and Morton's most formidable enemy (Gibbs to Morton, January 21, 1850; Historical Society of Pennsylvania).

In addition to being a Lutheran minister, Bachman was a naturalist of some note and, after 1831, a lifelong friend of John James Audubon. Members of the Literary and Philosophic Club of Charleston assigned the task of reviewing Nott's lectures to Reverend Bachman, who they knew had definite opinions on the subject of mankind's unity. Bachman was a Southerner and a slave owner, so it cannot be said that the battle was drawn along sectional lines or that Nott's arguments could be regarded as an apology for slavery.

Jean Louis Rodolphe Agassiz was another prominent scientist who entered the fractious argument with the parsons. He was born in 1807 at Moutier, Switzerland, of French parents, studied at several German universities, and, after 1846, became a professor at Harvard

University. There he worked as a zoologist and geologist and made extensive journeys, producing works on the animal world. Later, he was to popularize zoology in America and become an outspoken opponent of Darwinism. He died in 1873, the same year as Josiah Nott.

Of all Nott's friends in science, E. George Squier (1821–88) stands out. Squier was an archeologist of considerable note. He produced a pioneering work, with Dr. Edwin H. Davis, on the Mound Builders of the Mississippi Valley and has been referred to as the first *dirt* archeologist deserving of the name. He was largely self-educated and, after entering civil engineering and journalism, took a position in Chillicothe, Ohio. Squier settled in that particular area because he refused to live where there were slaves. His book on the Mound Builders became a classic first volume of memoirs of the series Contributions to Knowledge, published annually since 1848 by the Smithsonian Institute.

Squier learned of Nott through Morton, author of *Crania*, whereupon Squier wrote to Nott suggesting friendly collaboration on subjects of mutual interest. Nott replied two days later, saying, "…I shall be most happy to cultivate your friendship & to explore with you the fair field of truth & science…" At the time Nott wrote, he was five miles from his home, sitting up with a woman in labor. Rarely missing the opportunity to insert a point of humor, Nott informed Squier that, after all, "exploring a [pregnant] woman & a mound are pretty much the same" (August 19, 1848). In a subsequent letter, after Nott had been invited to give a lecture at Louisiana University, he joked that he would "…tell them all about…that infamous sinner Squier who has the hardihood to spout that the Indians were making potato hills in [the] Valley before Eve was convicted & punished for stealing apples" (September 20, 1848).

The most regrettable friendship that Nott was to attract from the ranks of science was with George Robins Gliddon (1809–57). Gliddon was the United States vice-consul at Cairo at the time Morton began correspondence with him. At Morton's request, Gliddon, with great zeal and enthusiasm, collected a large number of Egyptian skulls. When he first visited Egypt, he fell in love with the country and was anxious to return as soon as possible. He became the first to lecture to Americans on the subject of Egyptology. Although Gliddon had some saving graces, he is said to have been a name-dropper, a sponger, a swinger on the shirttails of the great, a braggart, and so on, says Stanton. Because of Gliddon's boorish behavior, Nott always complained about him in his letters.

Through his association with Morton, Gliddon came to know both Squier and Nott. Thus, Morton, Nott, Squier, Agassiz, and Gliddon composed a group that took the side of science in the battle of the parsons. Nott, to a large extent, was the spokesman for the group, and it was through his dedicated pen that the American School of Anthropology rose to a position of preeminence.

THE GEOLOGISTS

The growing science of geology comes into the picture toward the end of the eighteenth century and, in the nineteenth century, will play an important role in the evolutionary cause. Evolution, reasoned its champions, must have taken place over uncounted millions of years. The age of the planet, therefore, was crucial to the evolutionary argument, and it remained for the geologists to show the utter nonsense of Ussher's chronology.

This brief account of early geology begins with William Smith (1769–1839). Smith was for a number of years a surveyor of canals across central England. He was a man who loved his work, primarily because of his fascination with the fossils exposed in the beds through which the canals had been cut. As he examined the collections from different parts of the country, he gradually became aware that certain groups of fossils tended to occur in the same relative relationship to each other in these collections. He pursued his investigation along this line to the point where he was able to announce in 1799 that every formation, or stratum, had fossils peculiar to itself.

Fossils at one time had been regarded as the seeds of animals not yet come to life, or else forms placed in the rocks by the devil to distract man's attention from the true works of God. Gradually, however, many came to accept fossils as the remains of former types of life. For geologists they became a kind of Rosetta stone for the interpretation of Earth's history. But opinions on just how these formations of rock and fossils were to be interpreted varied greatly. The French biologist and pioneer geologist Cuvier is a case in point.

Georges (-Léopold-Chrétien-Frédéric-Dagobert) Cuvier was born in 1779 at Montbéliard and died of cholera during an epidemic that ravaged Europe in 1832. He came from a French Huguenot family that at one time had been subject to religious persecution. He gained the favor of Napoleon, and when the emperor died, Cuvier became the indisputable authority in the governmental spheres of science and education. His Protestantism did not seem to restrict Cuvier's acceptance. He even received promotion in the largely Roman Catholic France.

His investigations of the fossil record, especially the extinct forms of animals he discovered, brought Cuvier to face the question: What changes have taken place in the character of the Earth's surface that have caused the dissimilarity between the animal world of the past and that of the present? He concluded that there had been cataclysmic upheavals in the past that had destroyed animals who were now extinct and who existed only as fossil forms. He used as confirmation of his hypothesis the many legends of great floods, as in the Genesis account of Noah. *Perhaps* such occurrences as the *great flood* explained the disappearance of the mammoth and other great land animals living in Europe in earlier times.

Cuvier's hypothesis came to be known as the *catastrophe theory*, an explanation that was widely held into the nineteenth century. The popular version of this global destruction, an exaggeration of Cuvier's beliefs, was that in the past God had destroyed every living thing on Earth and, following this cataclysm, had created totally new forms of plants and animals. This devastation had occurred repeatedly, resulting in the geological discoveries of the likes of William Smith and Cuvier, of layer upon layer, or strata, of fossil remains. In contrast to the popular distortion of the catastrophe hypothesis, Cuvier pointed out that isolated parts of the planet may have been spared and that these living remnants had reproduced and reseeded the planet.

The Scotsman Charles Lyell (1797–1875), one of the greatest leaders in geology, is honored by many with the title father of *modern* geology. Lyell, imbued with a passion for nature study by his father, was attracted to William Smith's canal investigations early in his own career. He devoted the rest of his life to the study of geology in spite of poor eyesight. One source of comfort to Lyell, in the severe deprivation of poor vision that plagued him, was the fact that his wife with devoted self-sacrifice dedicated her life to helping him in his work. He undertook a number of long voyages of exploration, including a visit to Alabama because of his interest in fossils along the Alabama and Tombigbee rivers. Among other interesting finds, Alabama farmers had repeatedly plowed up the bones of long-extinct whales, from a time when most of the state was covered in water. While in Alabama, Lyell was hosted by Josiah Nott of Mobile, who wrote George Morton in February 1846 describing a long conversation he had with Lyell. Nott was very impressed with his visitor from England, but feared that he "is traveling so fast that he is taking up many false impressions & like all travelers I fear will write a good deal of trash..." Nott's words were, to some extent, prophetic since Lyell's *Principles of Geology* absolutely rejects the theory that the animal world in earlier ages consisted of entirely different species from those of modern times; the book declared that mammals and birds have existed from the very earliest of times. Lyell later rejected these extravagant claims and became an avid supporter of Darwin's theory of evolution.

Lyell's great service to the science of geology lies in his assertion that the phenomena of past ages should be explained on the basis of what is known from the present time. Thus, there are in the present age volcanoes, earthquakes, storms, and great upheavals of the earth that can explain much of the existing geologic formations. He therefore ruled out the cataclysmic theory of Cuvier in favor of more observable occurrences still going on. He argued that it is the upholders of the catastrophe theory whose duty it is to prove the correctness of their views.

CHARLES DARWIN

In June 1996, the Catholic News Service (CNS) reported a Vatican-sponsored conference on evolution and molecular biology. Interestingly, one of the participants referred to Charles Darwin as a "disguised friend of religion." The Rev. Arthur Peacocke, an Anglican theologian and biochemist, made this remark in all seriousness. Darwin's *The Origin of Species* may have disturbed religious leaders at the time of its publication in 1859, but more than a century later, evolution has opened the eyes of the faithful to the fact that biology is a creative process, "thus deepening their theological understanding." John Thavis of CNS described the key concept in the discussions as an "ongoing creation," a view, participants at the conference said, "that increasingly makes sense both scientifically and theologically." Father Stephen Happel, chair of the religion department at the Catholic University of America, said that these talks "were carving out a middle space between creationism and the godless scientific approach."

Charles Darwin (1809–82) was born, half a planet away, on the same day as Abraham Lincoln. Darwin was the son of a country doctor. His grandparents were distinguished figures of the eighteenth century. Darwin's paternal grandfather, Erasmus Darwin, was himself a naturalist, as well as a poet, and perceived that the farmers' selecting and crossing their livestock had important scientific implications. His maternal grandfather was Josiah Wedgwood, the virtual founder of the Staffordshire potteries and a pioneer in industrial-plant organization and product design. Of himself, Charles Darwin wrote in his autobiography that, "considering how fiercely I have been attacked by the Orthodox, it seems ludicrous that I once intended to be a clergyman." Thus, Josiah Nott in America and Charles Darwin in England, although their theories on human creation and descent were oceans apart, had in common the notoriety of being under attack by religious leaders.

Darwin's earth-shaking work began with a five-year voyage on the *H.M.S. Beagle,* on which he was employed as the ship's naturalist. He gathered specimens in large numbers. In 1860, some twenty-three years after he returned from this voyage, he published *The Origin of Species.* Twelve years later, he published *The Descent of Man.*

Having returned from his voyage on the *Beagle* in 1837 and then working on his finds for five years, Darwin allowed himself to speculate on the enormous volume of data he had collected and analyzed. Much later, in the Introduction to *The Origin of Species,* he writes:

> My work is now [1859] nearly finished; but as it will take me many more years to complete it, and as my health is far from strong, I have been urged to publish this abstract. I have more especially been induced to do this, as Mr. Wallace, who is now studying the natural history of the

Malay Archipelago, has arrived at almost exactly the same general conclusions that I have on the origin of species. In 1858 he sent me a memoir on this subject, with a request that I would forward it to Sir Charles Lyell, who sent it to the Linnean Society, and it is published in the third volume of the Journal of that Society. Sir C. Lyell and Dr. Hooker, who both knew of my work—the latter having read my sketch of 1844—honored me by thinking it advisable to publish, with Mr. Wallace's excellent memoir, some brief extracts from my manuscripts.

Not many people realize that the theory of evolution may be more accurately called the "Darwin-Wallace" theory, since the conclusions of Alfred Wallace were reached independently at about the same time as those of Darwin, and tend to corroborate the latter's research efforts. Darwin's observations led him to conclude that, although organisms reproduce prolifically, there remains a kind of steady state of numbers within a species. He concluded that there was a struggle for survival, often called *natural selection*—which Herbert Spencer (1820–1903) would later designate "survival of the fittest." This struggle, in turn, resulted in the continued existence of those forms most adapted to their environment. The variations that make such success possible are transmitted to the next generation genetically, thus resulting in an evolved species.

True understanding of the mechanism of evolution was not fully appreciated until modern genetics and gene mutations were more thoroughly researched in the twentieth century. It would take that long for the full implications of the pea-plant experiments of the Austrian monk Gregor Mendel (1822–84) to be understood. Some believed (Lamarck, for example) that evolution occurred through the inheritance of *acquired characteristics,* which in a narrow sense is true but not so in the broad sense. Some efforts were made to prove Lamarck's theory. In the process, many rodents lost their tails, victims of the investigator's scalpel, but never, not even once, was a tailless rat born to the severed-tailed parents.

As has been noted, Charles Lyell, in opposing the catastrophic hypothesis of Cuvier, set the stage for understanding the great age of the planet Earth. Lyell's geological views allowed time for evolution of species to occur. He therefore greatly influenced Charles Darwin in the formulation of his evolutionary work, as well as Thomas Malthus (1766–1834) in his studies of population.

The consequences of Darwin's evolutionary theory were that the universe and humankind could be viewed, not only as working its way toward a kind of preordained destiny through timeless species and structures, but also as moving along with no higher value or goal than *sheer survival*. Many saw in Darwin's work the greatest shock to human dignity since the jolting it took from the Copernican Revolution. Humanity might now be seen on a continual spectrum with the rest of the animal kingdom, including the lowest of living forms. At a stroke, it seemed, human civilization became the product of blind chance and galactic accident.

Under this interpretation of Darwin's theory, which Darwin himself never advanced, stability and reverence for the past would be displaced in favor of adaptation and experimentation. The *social Darwinists* saw justification in this for unchecked competition in the social and economic order. This outlook would serve the advantage, of course, of those already in power. On the other side were the so-called *instrumentalists,* who concluded that evolution represented a unique opportunity to choose the direction of evolution and thus improve the lot of all humankind.

Back in America, Josiah Nott was too intelligent, says Stanton (*The Leopard's Spots,* 185), to withhold his approval of a theory so well documented as that of Darwin's. The truth, it seemed, was that Darwin had beaten him at his own game "and outdone even Nott at infidelity." One of Darwin's most ardent supporters in America was Asa Gray, who saw no infidelity in the evolutionary theory. Asa Gray, a botanist and professor at Harvard, disagreed with Agassiz, his colleague at Harvard, and went on to take great pains to prove that Darwinism could be reconciled with belief in a personal God.

PIERRE TEILHARD DE CHARDIN

In reading the works of Teilhard de Chardin, it is not difficult to envisage this scientist-priest as one who loved the human race intensely. And the love that we see in him is by no means limited to the abstract. Father Teilhard risked his life many times to rescue or administer to the wounded during his four years as a stretcher-bearer with the French Army. He was born in Auvergne, France, in 1881 and died in New York in 1955. He was professor of geology at the Catholic Institute in Paris, director of the National Geologic Survey of China, and director of the National Research Center of France. He was a scientist, scholar, and, above all, a Jesuit priest. He placed no limitations on God. Rather, he sought for the truths of existence and the *becoming* of man with humility and dedication. His evolutionary vision is one that inspires the individual with thoughts of the greatness and beauty of creation. Julian Huxley, in his Introduction to Teilhard's *The Phenomenon of Man* (26), says:

> His influence of the world's thinking is bound to be important. Through his combination of wide scientific knowledge with deep religious feeling and a rigorous sense of values, he has forced theologians to view their ideas in the new perspective of evolution, and the scientists to see the spiritual implications of their knowledge. He has both clarified and unified our vision of reality. In the light of that new comprehension it is no longer possible to maintain that science and religion must operate in thought-tight compartments or concern separate sectors of life; they are both relevant to the whole of human existence.

One of the more salient aspects of Teilhard's view is that matter reveals itself to us in a state of becoming and that this genesis is marked by critical points at which evolution leaps to a higher plane. Associated with these evolutionary changes is "complexification," which results in a rise in consciousness that imparts direction and meaning to the entire process as it proceeds from the alpha (elementary particle state) towards its "omega point" or apogee.

The spirituality of Teilhard is thus rooted in his fascination with the cosmos. He saw in its great beauty the creative hand of God, not only as it existed for him, but as it was becoming for all humankind. In the *Divine Milieu*, Teilhard explains his belief in the dynamics of God's creation, as humanity seeks to cooperate spiritually in the destiny of the universe. His point of departure is to see God's creation in the *process of unfolding* and to make others see what conclusions are then forced upon them. These conclusions are brought out in his famous work *The Phenomenon of Man (POM)*.

To explain his view of evolution, Teilhard calls attention to the phenomenon of orthogenesis, a tendency for living things to change independent of external factors (although environment has its role to play in natural selection). Without this, he says, evolution would have been like an airplane that can taxi but never leave the ground. Without orthogenesis life would have only spread, but with it "there is an ascent of life that is invincible" (*POM,* 108, 109). It is through the order and essential unity of these factors, as well as a consequence of them, that the rise of consciousness begins. Thus, higher and higher forms of life progressively made their appearance throughout geologic history once the threshold from nonliving to living was crossed.

Then, out of this line of luxurious diversification and growth, there arose a line that favored increased brain size, and another critical point, a new threshold of consciousness, was at last reached. "To see life properly," writes Teilhard, "we must never lose sight of the unity of the biosphere that lies beyond the plurality and essential rivalry of individual beings" (112). This unity, as we see it from an evolutionary perspective, together with life's ascent and the rise in the level of consciousness, was to grow even more well-defined. In other words, in contrast to all the plurality and diversification of the lower species, the phenomenon that is humankind *converges*. Humankind, in fact, began the process of convergence long ago, while all other species continue to diversify.

Those who adopt the spiritual explanation are right, Teilhard reasons, when they defend so vehemently a certain transcendence of humanity over the rest of nature, but neither are the materialists wrong when they maintain that mankind represents "one further term in a series of animal forms." But at the same time if the threshold of reflection is really a critical transformation, as Teilhard so ardently believes—a mutation from zero to everything, as it were—he finds it impossible to imagine an intermediary individual at this precise level. The primordial unit of life, therefore, has finally become *somebody*. After the "grain of matter" comes the "grain of life," and lastly "we see constituted the *grain of thought*," so that, in the process, the Earth "gets a new skin," or better still, continues Teilhard, "it finds its soul" (*POM*, 183). Teilhard's lament, quoted at the beginning of this chapter, is remarkable for the insight it reveals. It relates mankind's reluctance to recognize that evolution has a precise *orientation* and a privileged *axis*. Weakened by this fundamental doubt, he says, "the forces of research are scattered, and there is no determination to build the earth" (*POM*, 142).

THE LIMITS OF SCIENCE

It is with Teilhard de Chardin, and others like him, that history begins to reveal itself as a process of growth and maturity. We see in Teilhard's works a genuine reverence for all of creation, as well as a vivid picture of humankind's attempts to understand it. He invited science and religion to come together, to combine their efforts in a grand new undertaking. What caused the separation in the past is of no consequence now. What is important in this day and age is for religion and science to again join forces, as in the ancient past, but without the possessiveness that characterized the ancient system. Let the one partner inform the other instead of each coveting the power of dominance, one over the other. As Teilhard would say, such acquisitiveness must come to an end if we are to build the earth.

There is evidence in this century that a new common mentality, a changed Zeitgeist, is replacing the more vitriolic conflict between science and religion. The dialectic has become more productive, more useful, in reaching the goal of a final synthesis between these two vital interests. There is yet a long road to travel, of course, but we can see the beginnings of a reconciliation. The pillows of the marriage bed are ready for the ancient partners (science and religion) to again rest their heads: the tax collector Zacchaeus has climbed the sycamore tree to better see Jesus coming down the road (Luke 19:5).

Strangely, it may seem, astronomy, the science that first engendered the revolutionary rift, is the very discipline that seems to now encourage the reconciliation. In *The End of Science: Facing the Limits of Knowledge in the Twilight of the Scientific Age,* John Horgan, a senior writer for *Scientific American* magazine, promotes the idea that science has gone about as far as it can in answering fundamental questions, such as *How did the universe begin?* and *How did life begin?* In other words, science and theology have reached a nexus, a boundary across which scientists and religious leaders are reaching out to one another. All scientists may not express this new relationship as I have, but one can hardly read a book dealing with cosmic origins that is not, at the same time, infused with God-talk. Practically speaking, there is about as much theology in some of these books as there is science.

Yes, scientists are dabbling more and more in theology not so much by choice as by necessity. They have reached a point in their discussions in which they no longer avoid the most fundamental of all eternal questions: *Why is there something rather than nothing?* God-talk in science is all but unavoidable. The objective is to find that middle ground between unbending creationism and godless evolution. These two extreme positions are integral to the problem. Indeed, they are two among the legion of demons that have thrust themselves into the marriage bed of science and religion. Such as these are keeping the two greatest endeavors of humankind apart from one another. The opposing forces of the extreme positions may seem beyond the realm of healthy dialogue because their intractable hostility never abates. Dislike them as we may, however, the extremists of the world do play a role in the overall strategy of God. The demons are among us for a very good reason and that is to demonstrate to humankind the perilous distance we must travel before free choice leads us in the direction that the Creator intends for us.

CONVERGENCE AND UNITY

Looking back today over the twelve delightful years that I spent on this richly rewarding enterprise, I find that its result for me has been its confirmation of a thought I have long and faithfully entertained: of the unity of the race of man, not only in its biology but also in its spiritual history…irresistibly advancing to some kind of mighty climax, out of which the next great movement will emerge.
—Joseph Campbell, on completion of *The Masks of God*

The whole idea of convergence, the positive force of the historical superego, is a conclusion drawn from the observation of biological and intellectual patterns. We can see these patterns as they develop against a background of seemingly haphazard experiments of nature. This drawing together of scattered elements and giving them direction can be observed especially in the phylogenetic development of humanity itself.

The story begins in the distant zoological past when the first living things came into being. These primitive forms began as the simplest of molecular structures capable of growth and reproduction. Some of these tiny elements, sensing their chemical affinities (not through any thought process because they had no nervous system), began to collect and amass into slightly larger units, becoming such microscopic miracles of nature as the *euglena*, the *amoeba,* and the *paramecium*—single-celled members of the subkingdom Protozoa. So there came to be a primordial convergence even in these early stages of biological existence. But the possibilities for advance were limited in these primitive forms because single-cell organisms such as these reproduce by cleavage of the parent-cell into two daughter-cells. This biological process results in nearly complete destruction of the body pattern, thereby necessitating a rebuilding of it in the two daughter-cells.

Eventually some of these unicellular organisms, guided by an unseen hand in the chemistry of creation, began congregating into multicellular organisms like the sponges (the phylum *Porifera*). This multicellular advance allowed for greater differentiation of the cellular units into separate functional components, dividing the labor of food gathering and reproduction, and creating greater efficiency in the living unit. The process of natural affinities continued to form more-complex organisms. Eventually some of the cellular components differentiated into primitive neural cells. As miniscule as this first nervous system may have been, it constituted the primordial beginnings of consciousness, yet to unfold but potentially there nonetheless.

Having mentioned these things in passing, there is no need here to dwell on more examples of convergence among the lower biological forms since our primary interest is in humanity. Suffice it to say that many pages could be filled in further explication of this phenomenon. We now move on to the study of the history of consciousness.

THE CONVERGENCE OF HUMANKIND

If one stands aside and attempts to look at humanity from the point of view of an impartial observer, what one sees is a complex anthropological phenomenon. So alike in many ways to the other primates, humankind is separated from its closest living relatives by an ocean of potential, a sea of reflection, and a worldwide landscape of inventiveness and creativity. Every nonhuman member of the animal kingdom shows a pattern of diversity that, like a fan, spreads its leaves out in a vast semicircle among the other spheres of living things. Here and there a node will appear on one of the leaves of the fan, and from this nodal point a change in the direction of genetic energy occurs, bringing forth yet another diverse array. The new array, in turn, gives rise to a multitude of new species. Sponges are a good example of one of these nodal points. Its progenitors, having converged into a multicellular life-form, burst forth at a higher level with another display of incomparable experiments in the diversity of living organisms.

Convergence and Unity

Some anthropologists believe the evidence for human evolution begins with the fossil remains of *Australopithecus,* an erect, bipedal primate who lived on the African continent some four to five million years ago. Even here, there was a diversity of species, a spreading out from the nodal energy on the primate tree of some now-extinct line, before the *Australopithecus* finally became extinct itself over a million years ago.

In the final analysis, it does not matter what happened during these very early times, at least not insofar as concerns the present discussion. What is significant, however, is the presence of *a single species only* of modern man *(Homo sapiens)*. Speaking generally, any person on any continent and of any race can interbreed with any other person and produce fertile offspring. For our purposes, let that be the definition of "species." Horses and donkeys can interbreed, for example, but their offspring (mules) are sterile. The horse and the donkey, therefore, are different species. There was a time in our earlier Western history when some anthropologists (ethnologists) believed the black man and the white man to be separate species (see previous chapter). We know now that this misguided assumption was false.

Thus, humankind occupies a unique position in the animal kingdom. Fish, birds, reptiles, and so on, exist in the animal kingdom as myriads of species, whereas the genus *Homo,* which at one time consisted of multiple species, presently exists as a single species. Humanity, therefore, if examined as a member of the animal kingdom, shows virtually indisputable evidence of convergence. The races, many think, are a comparatively late development in the anthropological story of humankind. It is as if, by sheer genetic energy, the forces of creation made one last desperate try at species diversification, but, overcome by the forces of convergence, failed in the attempt. The races of humankind will never disappear in our lifetime, perhaps never completely pass away at all, but there is good evidence, culturally and intellectually at least, that racial distinctions are slowly disappearing.

The law of convergence spills over into the thinking world as well, the sphere of the human mind, or what Teilhard de Chardin calls the *noosphere.* We see, therefore, that humanity has turned its exceptional intellect in upon itself as it reflects on its purposes and origins; it has entered a field of attractive forces unparalleled in the vast zoological spectrum in which it is immersed. In the momentous

47

process of folding in upon itself, humankind does not rise simply to give birth to another nodal point from which it will again fan out in divergent, dead-end forays. Rather, this radical change in the fledgling phenomenon of reflection has given rise to a new form of inheritance. Although still unquestionably necessary, the role of DNA in inheritance is just a part of the burgeoning human story. Now, in addition to the chemical libraries of the body—the chromosomal and mitochondrial DNA—humanity also inherits the libraries of the world, a vast communications network, jet air-travel, radio, television, the Internet, and on and on.

We have become a worldwide, superhuman organism made up of individuals and bound together by the inventiveness of the human intellect. This new birthright applies to literature, the arts, and an immense storehouse of cultural traditions, as well as the sciences. We continue to build upon these treasures as we stand on the shoulders of the great pioneers who preceded our times. Without our intellectual and religious traditions, our world of libraries, our complex system of communications, and more, we would fall back to the days before Cro-Magnon man. It is as though human individuals have repeated the *Porifera* experiment, bursting forth at a higher level, only on a vastly greater scale, one that involves the intellect rather than biological principles alone. We are not physically contiguous, of course, like the multicellular sponges, but we are bound together, nevertheless, as individuals participating in a fledgling, supraorganic entity, not quite sure of its immense power, hesitant to take its first steps, scarcely aware of its new identity, and precariously teetering at the pinnacle of all the other palaces of nature. This is not mere poetic speculation. For many years, investigators worldwide have been actively trying to define the existence and nature of the "global consciousness." (See http://noosphere.princeton.edu. If the Web site is no longer under that URL, search the Net for "Global Consciousness Project.")

This new manner of inheritance on the global level by no means forces aside the legacy of the reproductive cells. Indeed, our greatest problem, it seems, is the persistence of our phylogenetic savagery. We are fascinated by violence and devastation, entertained by treachery and duplicity, and bored to tears by honesty and candor. We may try to repress our interest in such things and end up morose to the point of psychosis, or give them free reign and vent terror upon our neighbors. We have reached a critical point in our development that forces us to recognize our feral tendencies and to deal with them in a salutary way or have them erupt from the subconscious where they have been so conveniently packed away. This is not a problem of simple arrogance. It is rather a condition of denial because in this predicament humankind fails to recognize its basic frailty, its dependency on the persistence of divine succor. Recognition of this dependency allows humankind to draw strength from weakness, as did the apostle Paul, rather than count it as failure (2 Cor 12:10).

THE CONVERGENCE OF THE INTELLECT

I am privileged to have witnessed intellectual convergence in the course of my seventy-five years. During this time I have participated in the world of scientific wonders and seen their development in terms of a definite pattern. I see this development as another purposeful intervention of God in the affairs of creation. I see also in the historical pattern of the intellect the undeniable evidence that science was not given to us for our comfort alone, or for our self-destruction, but to help us find our way through creation itself.

Humankind sits at the pinnacle of the biological world because of its superior intellect. We have seen how convergence works vis-à-vis its somatic manifestation, but the brain of the body is like the hardware of a computer. It cannot really function properly without sensory input. That is, as in the computer analogy, it must have the software (sensory) input if it is to do anything other than simply vegetate. Turning inward, then, we take the next step, to see where we are headed intellectually. I have mentioned above the role of science and human traditions in shaping the "thinking world," the noosphere, but I have not discussed how convergence has occurred in the context of our intellectual history. Here we can see the scattered elements of intellectual diversity more clearly because they have fanned out and converged again within historical times. As to the phenomenon of convergence, we do not need to examine any fossils because, in this case, the process is right in front of us, staring us in the face.

The object of the human intellect, that which it seeks as its fulfillment, is knowledge. There are degrees and kinds of knowledge with which human beings concern themselves. In the attempt at a greater understanding of all things, we naturally reach out beyond our mere physical surroundings because human curiosity is not satisfied by the material alone. We seek understanding, particularly self-understanding, through the knowledge of all that is presented to the intellect, spiritual as well as physical. Aristotle could comprehend almost all there was to know about his historical times, and, indeed, Aristotle has been regarded as a universal genius. He knew and understood such subjects as medicine, ethics, politics, poetics, rhetoric, meteorology, mineralogy, natural science, physics, and metaphysics, and that's just a partial list. He was a student of Plato, another famous philosopher of antiquity, and the teacher of one of the most famous military leaders of all time, Alexander the Great.

However, as scientific interests expanded and more new discoveries were made, another Aristotle became impossible. No longer could one person know everything there was to know, or even come close to the notion of a universal genius. Philosophy, which once embodied all knowledge, became broken up into so many "anthills" of intellectual pursuits, or what might be termed disciplines. As such, each discipline worked away at its own small sphere of interest, with hardly any communication between the various neighboring efforts. Thus, the field of biology had little to do with the discipline of mathematics or even chemistry. There was, of course, an inkling that biology and chemistry were somehow related, but the nature of this relationship escaped the individual scientists as they each buried themselves deeper and deeper into their own isolated realm of expertise. It was as if each scholar worked with a set of blinders on; every little "ant hill" was a separate and distinct entity.

But then, as inevitably happens, each discipline grew and grew until it began to touch, and finally fuse with, its neighbor. Scientists involved in the study of biology and in the study of chemistry, for example, began to understand that their respective disciplines had a great deal in common, and the science of biochemistry was born. The discipline of biochemistry, therefore, is a common ground where biologists and chemists can meet and understand one another.

There was still a long way to go before the artificial boundaries between biology and chemistry would be completely erased. Chemists (or, in this case, biochemists) concerned themselves with the unseen events that took place in chemical reactions, while biologists "lived" in a world of the visible and the dissectible. The biologist took his animal material and dissected it layer by layer in order to understand how the organism functioned, or he studied the living animal in its natural habitat. The biochemist, on the other hand, had to grind everything up, even to dissolve the biological material in some kind of solvent, to get at its chemical nature. Eventually, the biochemist would tell the biologist that living tissue contains all kinds of fascinating things such as enzymes, hormones, amino acids, proteins, fats, and sugars. The molecules known as DNA (deoxyribonucleic acid), responsible for the genetic mechanisms of the organism, and RNA (ribonucleic acid), the substance necessary to make proteins from amino acids, were very interesting discoveries by chemists. But where did they fit in with what biologists knew about the animals they were observing and dissecting? Did these things have a place in the body?

To be sure, all major biochemical events have a definite place in the body. The precise location of these biochemicals in the living organism was made known through the contributions of another discipline, namely, the science of physics. Through research into the nature of light and optics, considered to be within the purview of physics, the microscope was invented: first the light microscope, and much later, the more powerful electron microscope. With these instruments, especially the electron microscope, it became possible to locate with great precision many important biochemical events. Anatomy, an integral part of biology, was no longer limited to the grossly visible specimen. With the light microscope, the cell—the basic building block of complex organisms—became known, and the science of microscopic anatomy was born. Even more significant, however, with the electron microscope the visualization of biochemical molecules, such as DNA, became a reality. With the advent of these sophisticated instruments, the artificial boundary separating chemistry from biology has all but disappeared.

The same may be said of the other scientific disciplines. Mathematics, never far removed from any of the sciences, became integral to them all, especially physics. These boundaries—really human constructs separating mathematics, physics, physiology, biology, and chemistry—were all, in a manner of speaking, obliterated. Even sciences such as geology and history, which at first glance might seem to have nothing to do with biology and chemistry, came to depend on these and the other sciences to move beyond even the crudest levels of investigation.

What the human race is witnessing in the human intellect, therefore, is the simple and unavoidable fact of *convergence*. The pattern is obvious, but what is the world of science (and, in fact, all human knowledge) converging toward? This seems to present humankind with questions of paramount importance: What is the ultimate destiny of the human race and, for that matter, all of the physical universe? Where are we going as a people? What is the ultimate destiny of *Homo religiosus*?

Religion and science are partners in reaching the final goal we have been discussing. We as a species are converging, but converging toward what? Convergence is pressing in on religion as well as on science. It may not *seem* to be the case, especially if a person lives in one of the regions of violent religious intolerance. But this is all a part of the seminal dialectic discussed earlier, the sputtering, coughing engine of history that is leading humankind toward some distant goal. Despite this, religion and science, seen as partners in interpreting reality, cannot come together effectively until the scattered elements of religion have successfully dealt with their own factional diaspora. The dialectic between science and religion cannot do its work as long as the religious communities continue to writhe with violence and bitterness against one another.

There are questions for which there can be no experimental answers: What preceded the big bang? What is the ultimate energy source that holds subatomic particles together? What is human consciousness? Now that science is beginning to reach these limits, I believe scientists will start looking to theologians for more answers, tentative ones, of course, for which they have no hope of answering themselves. I do not mean that science will accept theological solutions to scientific problems. What I do mean is that, as science reaches the limits of its empirical method, it will be drawn to theology out of necessity, if not respect, and perhaps both. It is important for science to explore its limits and not be defeated by them. Indeed, to critically examine the interface at which science and theology study each other, where physics and metaphysics may be seen as contiguous, seems a legitimate scientific pursuit, even if it does have theological overtones.

For example, science might ask religion, "What kind of deity is your God? Tell me and perhaps I too can believe in your God. How does your God interact with material existence? Can your God suddenly make a chaotic existence out of a rational one? What are miracles? Can and does God break the laws of nature in, say, the case of a miracle? What is free will, if indeed it really exists? How can God be present in human history without destroying human freedom? Why does your God allow such suffering if your belief is in a loving, personal God?

"Can you see," continues the scientist, "that I might like to join forces with you if only I knew what you mean by religion. I don't want to buy a pig in a poke any more than you do. Why can't your theologians agree on these things? How can you expect me to have any inclination to respect what you believe if you yourself don't know what you believe? You say I must have *faith*. Please don't ask me to pray if I don't believe in a God that hears prayers."

I don't know that we will ever achieve a world consensus on the answers to the above, or what the answers—even what the questions might mean to each individual. Certainly we are taught by history that divine revelations come to a people within their particular cultural context. Perhaps religious diversity, to a certain extent, *is* to be desired. Nobody wants to be a carbon copy of the other guy, but at the same time humanity must strive to grow and mature in its religious outlook (regardless of culture), and always have a task before it. Stagnation and self-satisfaction are among the worst enemies of religious rapprochement.

But there is a common ground that world religions can aspire to, and I believe it is one that most scientists can accept, even the ones who are the most distrustful of religious influences. It is the common ground that starts with a basic trust in reality. It is a first step that must be taken, I believe, because it follows along a path of what is good for our growth and maturity, toward a truly authentic existence as human creatures.

There is yet another important relationship, or interface, between science and religion, namely, the *arts*. Great works of art have inspired humanity down through the ages, but what is their relationship to science and religion? Is there something one can learn about reality through the eyes of the artist? Do these works indeed reflect the image of God in their creative force? Or could they simply be another product of a sophisticated machine, the conglomeration of bones and biochemicals that some would describe as the human essence? In other words, is there something really *special* about these most wonderful of artistic endeavors? Do they provide us with another kind of insight into what it is to be authentically human? As I have said, I believe each of us is a work of art, an ongoing composition that begins at birth and does not end until the day we die. As one of God's creatures, we are a work in progress. Therefore, we should sing our song and tell our story. I believe that something inside of us compels us to do so.

5

THE GLORIFICATION OF SCIENCE THROUGH ART

> From sense, memory is produced, but from repeated remembrance of the same thing, we get experience, for many remembrances in number constitute one experience. From experience, however, the universal now established in the soul, the one beside the many which is a single unit within them all, the principle of art and science arises: if it is conversant with coming-to-be you have art; if with being, it is science. —Aristotle, *Posterior Analytics*

The arts are so intimately bound up with science that it is difficult to imagine a boundary that separates them. Science analyzes artistic creations by its special methods, although it can never explain the emotional impact of great art on the observer. Science can explain the chemistry of the pigments and examine the brush strokes on the painter's canvas, yet it can make no claim to understand the artist's intent or inspiration. The science of harmonics examines tonal qualities of a musical composition but can never define, or in any way explain, its aesthetic value. Thus, science meets with its limits in the arts, just as it meets its limits in the universe of matter and energy. It is only insofar as the arts relate to the material universe, of course, that science has any role to play in their understanding. Beyond that rather mundane role, science must bow to the unknown and the unexplained, and that is the point at which the philosophy of aesthetics comes into the picture. It is another case where mystery and the supernatural beckon to us on the other side of an interface in reality, where the physical properties of matter end and their metaphysical extensions begin.

Faith Seeking Understanding

In Greek mythology it was the Muses, the nine goddesses and daughters of the gods Zeus and Mnemosyne, who were said to inspire artists. Even among ancient pagans there was the sense that great art transcended human capabilities of analysis. It had to be *inspired* by the gods. Aristotle distinguished science from art on the basis of *being* (science) and *coming-to-be* (art). He said that "art imitates nature," which is not to say the same thing as his teacher, Plato, who insisted that nature itself is an imitation of a reality beyond human sensibility. When Aristotle spoke of art as an imitation, however, he was more definitive than Plato in his assertion that art partly completes what nature cannot bring to a finish. Thus, said Aristotle, "experience is a knowledge of singulars whereas art is of universals" (Aristotle, *Metaphysics* I. 1, 981a).

Plotinus, a third-century philosopher and Neoplatonist, gave far more importance to art than did Plato. In Plotinus's view, art raises the soul to contemplate the universal, thereby touching the divine principle, or as he called it, "the one." The contemplation of art is therefore likened to a mystical experience in which one loses oneself in the magnificence of the aesthetic composition. From Plotinus into the Middle Ages, art became a method of religious expression, but in many cases this was because the subject and imagery of the work itself dealt with religious themes.

Like Plato, the nineteenth-century German philosopher Arthur Schopenhauer believed that forms exist beyond worldly experience, and that aesthetic satisfaction is achieved by contemplating art forms for their own sakes. Most of life, believed Schopenhauer, consists of functioning on a zoological-economical-political level of concern. Even the intellect is in the service of the will to live, "serving merely as means for the preservation of the individual and his species." But in the arts it is possible to view an object in terms other than its relationship to the well-being of the viewer. The "world eye," as Schopenhauer called it, allows one to lose oneself to desire, fear, and the vicissitudes of mortality in space and time, and even the laws of cause and effect, which operate in this domain (Joseph Campbell, *Creative Mythology*, 81).

PURPOSEFUL ART

The kind of art that I am *not* talking about are paintings that commemorate historical events or music that inspires piety or patriotism. Plato would banish certain types of art from his ideal society because he thought they encouraged immorality or portrayed base characters. Aristotle saw in the Greek tragedy a great stimulus for the emotions, especially those of pity and fear, which he considered morbid and unhealthful. Yet, by the end of the play the spectator is emotionally exhausted and thereby purged of his or her unhealthy fears. This type of catharsis makes the audience psychologically healthier and more capable of happiness. This is the type of effect Adela Yarbro Collins sees in apocalyptic literature, particularly as it relates to the biblical book of Revelation. The thesis of her book *Crisis and Catharsis: The Power of the Apocalypse* is that John of Patmos, in view of Christian oppression under the Roman emperor Domitian, wrote the Apocalypse with this purpose in mind.

To me, purposeful art also includes, besides the Greek tragedies, religious paintings and religious musical compositions. This is not to say that a religious painting cannot be inspirational, but in this type of art it is not always easy to separate the emotions evinced by the painting itself from the emotions evinced from the religious theme it depicts. That is to say, the religious painting points to something other than the work of art in such a way as to deflect the viewer's thoughts from what is before him or her, sometimes forcing the observer to contemplate the message or subject depicted, rather than the work itself.

It is the same with any great musical composition that gets its impetus from a religious theme. J. S. Bach's *Mass in B-Minor* serves as a good example of this type of artistic work. This particular piece is a favorite of mine, and I am deeply moved every time I listen to its plaintive chords and the beautiful voices of the chorus. Yet it has as its central impetus a reflection of a meaningful religious ritual. To what extent, therefore, am I moved almost to tears in contemplation of the Eucharistic sacrifice, its historical origins in the crucifixion of Christ, or, by contrast, the music itself? It is most difficult in such instances to separate out these intense emotions and attribute them to one thing or the other. That is not to say that the *B-Minor Mass* has no value simply as a work of art independent of its subject, or the original impetus for its composition, because it most certainly does.

ART FOR ART'S SAKE

It is not my intent to belittle the functions of art as alluded to in the examples above, and yet I do believe there are purer art forms that show a kind of inspiration that is inimitable. It is this art form, unblemished by designed messages or special meanings, to which I now refer. I do not speak lightly of my appreciation and love of the arts, particularly that of great music. I say "great" music or "great" works of art, because not all objects that are called "art" are capable of evincing the type of emotive dimensions of which I am speaking here.

From this point on, the entire field of aesthetics becomes more complicated. Most philosophers (and psychologists) have an opinion on the arts, but the idea that stands out boldly in all the discussions is that there is something in the arts that escapes human efforts to explain or understand. Great works of art are infused with mystery because they can move us to emotional dimensions that transcend the ordinary. In this I agree completely with Schopenhauer. One can never understand what this mystical thing is because one can never examine the mind of the artist for the origins of that creative force, that spark of inspiration and imagination where it all begins. The artist, even as the creative agent, can never fully understand it in his or her work, much less can one who does not directly experience the gestation period and eventual birth of the aesthetic creation. Inspiration like this just happens, it seems, perhaps even rising out of an archetypical existence, the true reality, of which Plato speaks, yet which is somehow embedded in the collective unconscious of us all. This could be one reason that great works of art move us so deeply—they remind us of an untouched reality within our own psyche. Perhaps for one blissful moment we embrace a truth at the very core of our being, recognizing it as something far more precious than all the material advantages we can imagine or ever bring to consciousness.

I am not a professional musician, or critic, or artist in any creative or performing sense, but I have built two harpsichords and have a great appreciation of music, particularly the classics. In addition to my love of the baroque and classical periods, I have a particular fondness for Beethoven's works. As I was driving along recently, I happened to tune in on a performance of Beethoven's *Fourth Piano Concerto*. I tried to look at this great work from a scientific viewpoint. What is it in this concerto—aside from a lot of sounds, notes of different harmonic qualities, tones, and overtones—that makes it such a wondrous composition? It is not simply a bunch of notes put together in a certain order. It has no religious or mystical message, either in the title or the performance itself. So what is it that gave me such great pleasure that moved me to soar emotionally beyond the finitude of an earthly existence?

I believe that the emotions I experienced, as I drove along in my car, were close to those experienced by the composer himself as he wrote the piece. I believe that for a moment I was touched by the same inspiration that moved Beethoven to compose this great work of art. And I cannot put aside the conviction that both Beethoven and, through his experience, myself were brushed ever so tenderly by the creative force of God's own divinity.

I suppose what I am saying is that I agree with Plotinus, for in that moment I was united with "the One," whether as some kind of divine principle within myself, or as a kind of infusion in the transcendental sense. I would have to also agree with Schopenhauer that in those moments of shared inspiration, we escape beyond the world of mundane experiences. Thus, we are elevated by some means to a new level of existence. Regardless of what actually "happened" while I was listening in my car, I am not alone in feeling these deep emotions upon hearing or viewing great works of art. I may be in the minority, however, as to my particular interpretation of the phenomenon.

I remember a strikingly meaningful discussion between a concert artist and a radio host that occurred between performances. The question arose as to whether great musical compositions inspired people to do good things. The artist responded by pointing out that there were Nazi officers at a certain concentration camp who could be moved to tears by a Mozart symphony, and in the next moment order the execution of thousands of Jews. As tragic as this story is, I do not think it changes what has been said about the forces of inspiration and their divine origins.

Christians believe, as did the ancient Israelite prophets (see the Book of Hosea), that God is always seeking to turn the sinner back to the ways of righteousness. The hidden God calls out to us in many ways and in many forms, including divinely inspired, great works of art. Earlier I made the point that God remains invisible for a very good reason. Certainly a visible God whom humanity was cognizant of, and who watched our every move, would limit our freedom and our faith. This is not the kind of divinity God is. God influences us through other means that do not thwart our religious faith. Indeed, God calls us to unity with the divine principle of the universe in such a way as to *increase* faith, rather than diminish it. Beautiful music and other forms of art are just one example of this self-communication of God.

A CELEBRATION OF PARTNERSHIP

When we hear a beautiful piece of music, it strikes me that the performance itself is a celebration of an ideal partnership of science and religion. Enough has been said in the way of differences between science and religion vis-à-vis the arts. It is also useful, I believe, to show how they complement one another in and through the arts. I will use examples of this partnership as viewed from the perspective of the performing arts.

The Stradivari family did not build their remarkable violins, renowned throughout the world, without a great deal of labor, trial and error, and what is essentially scientific experimentation, though it would never be called that. In the same way, no musical instrument of high quality ever comes to be without an enormous scientific effort. Surely, there is a lot of love, patience, and artistic appreciation that is also required to make these wonderful instruments, but the love of good music is by no means enough to do the job. Most of the artists I have met would not know how to construct a flute, much less something as complicated as a piano.

The modern piano is actually the end product of a long process of evolution, from harp to harpsichord to the Steinway. The harpsichord is basically a harp with a keyboard, such that the strings are plucked by depressing keys rather than plucking them directly with the fingertips. Most harpsichords look like the piano, except that the width of the keyboard is narrower. If one looks inside the instrument, however, one can observe that the strings are plucked by a thin piece of plastic (in Bach's time it was carved quill) called a plectrum. When the key of the harpsichord is depressed, it acts as a lever to lift the plectrum, causing it to "pluck" the string.

I love the sound of a good harpsichord and much prefer it to the piano in the performance of keyboard works written before the piano came into existence. One can perform on the piano any work written for the harpsichord, but it just does not sound as it should. On the other hand, there are definite limitations to the harpsichord, such that one should never attempt a Beethoven sonata, for example, on the earlier instrument. Beethoven wrote his keyboard works after the piano was invented to take advantage of this instrument's pianoforte (soft and loud) capabilities. A harpsichord can only pluck the string, and once it is plucked, that is all the sound one gets out of the string. A piano, by contrast, instead of plucking the strings, has a complicated lever system that causes a felt covered "hammer" to strike the strings. The advantage of this hammer-strike is that the harder the key is depressed the louder the sound that is produced as the strings are impacted.

I am making the point here more tediously than I intended, but what I am saying is that a lot of experimentation and labor of love went into the making of the first pianos, as well as their more sophisticated successors. It required not only good craftsmanship to build the first generation of pianos, but good science as well. The science of levers and their applications is about as basic to physics as one can get. And yet, had it not been for someone who saw the potential for pianos from the artistic viewpoint, these marvelous instruments would never have been invented.

The inspired artist, then, saw in the potential of the piano a new and more profound way to express the artistic visions that cried out from the depths of one's being. This new inspiration suggested nuances of sound and feeling incapable of expression on the older instrument, the harpsichord. Inspiration such as this demands to be born out of some unknown and mysterious source within the psyche. It is an ineffable force that transcends, while it transforms, artist and listener alike. It is without doubt an experience of the numinous, the sense of "the holy" that is evoked by the great works of art (Otto, *The Idea of the Holy*).

But as profound and wonderful as the wellsprings of artistic inspiration might be, the creative dream can never become a reality in the absence of science. The artist, using the skills of composition and the tools of musical science, brings to bear his creative energies in a truly original work of art, something no one has ever heard before. In this effort, building on the works of his forebears, he nevertheless advances the storehouse of creativity for all humankind, and in so doing, demonstrates the hidden powers of the *imago Dei*. That God creates in a more fundamental way than his human creatures is not to be disputed. But because we are created in the image of God, we are allowed to share in that miraculous creative wellspring.

If these views seem reasonable, then science and the arts, the natural and the supernatural, the earthly and the divine, beckon to us along the interface of reality's dimensions. It says to us: Behold my magnificence and you will understand what you are more clearly. Be exposed to the whole of reality and become more authentically human. See how existence fits together and catches a glimpse of the wholeness of reality. Comprehend your role in the struggle of creation and find creative fulfillment in yourself. Discover who you are and be immersed in God's love. Read what God has written on your heart, and be what you already are.

6

MEDICINE, MAGIC, AND THE HIDDEN GOD

> Now as he was going along and approaching Damascus, suddenly a light from heaven flashed around him. He fell to the ground and heard a voice saying to him, "Saul, Saul, why do you persecute me?" He asked, "Who are you, Lord?" The reply came, "I am Jesus, whom you are persecuting. But get up and enter the city, and you will be told what you are to do." The men who were traveling with him stood speechless because they heard the voice but saw no one. Saul got up from the ground, and though his eyes were open, he could see nothing; so they led him by the hand and brought him into Damascus.   —Acts 9:3–8

A physician-friend once told me he believed that Paul's experience on the road to Damascus was caused by a temporal lobe seizure. He was proposing a possible medical explanation for Paul's conversion experience, including not only the described fall to the ground and the blindness, but, by inference, the "voice from heaven" as well. I got the impression at the time, although I did not pursue the point, that this medical explanation, at least to my friend's way of thinking, negated the reality of Paul's conversion experience.

For some reason the memory of that incident has remained very clear, and I replay in my own mind the full implications of what my friend said. In those days, some thirty-five years ago, I may have been tempted to argue against his conclusion that Paul actually experienced a seizure. In other words, there was a time in my life that I might have perceived the medical explanation of Paul's conversion experience, valid or not, as a threat to my Christian faith. I now see

63

the whole incident as a degree of immaturity on my part, and as a great lesson in what is wrong with our present-day perception of the proper relationship between science and religion.

Does it really matter, in fact, whether the apostle had a seizure or not at the time of his conversion? Should we limit God to working through humans in a certain preconceived way? Indeed, is it not possible for God to work in and through his human subjects by naturally occurring, physical means, or is it necessary for God to manifest some "miraculous" event, such as light and voices from heaven? Obviously, we will never know if Paul actually experienced a seizure, but it makes no difference in the final analysis.

Let us suppose that we could go back in time, place upon Paul's head (unnoticed by the apostle himself) a minuscule and supersensitive encephalographic device, and then actually record this hypothetical seizure. Would it make any difference regarding whether or not Paul also experienced a revelation from God at that particular moment? The immediate reaction of a great many might be this: "Paul just *thought* he had a revelation from God, but the fact of the seizure explains everything." Thus, they would continue, some with gleeful smugness: "The most profound theology in all the New Testament began from a simple cerebrocortical event." Historians of medicine would undoubtedly write volumes about how the apostle's unfortunate medical condition changed the entire course of Western history. One can also pose similar questions and objections about other New Testament events. Were the unclean spirits (demons) that Jesus cast out (Mark 1:23–26; 5:13) really supernatural possessions, just an ordinary illness, or perhaps no real physical ailment at all? Were the "lepers" that Jesus made clean really lepers? Was the leprosy of first-century Judea the same as the Hansen's disease of the present day? Did Jesus actually cure anybody of any real (physical) illness? One could ask such questions ad nauseam, and many do, because they are the "bread and butter" questions of historical criticism. Biblical scholars ask these kinds of questions not because they are doubters (although some may be), but because they desire a better understanding of the historical times in which Jesus lived. Others seem to ask them in order to discredit the Christian faith, pure and simple.

Much as some might prefer that science and religion be cordoned off from one another representing separate and unrelated realities, as it were, there are no grounds for such wishful thinking. Science and religion have been intertwined—bedfellows since the dawn of history—with all the conflicts and mutual attraction the metaphor implies. As in any ideal marriage, the two partners have grown and matured as a result of their encounters with each other. These growth spurts have occurred not always in spite of, but mostly because of, the conflicts. And both gathered their forces within a milieu of fear, violence, and priestly arrogance, and both with magic as their handmaiden.

DEMONS AND GODS

Diseases were demons in ancient civilizations, unclean spirits. The gods were tricky, arbitrary, and powerful. In the beginning the priest or shaman wielded the power, convincing the masses that he had the inside track to a special deity, or that he alone possessed the secret herbs that would expel demons. In those days neither science nor religion held sway over the other because there was really little difference between them, certainly none that was well-defined. The Babylonians had their demons, herbs, and incantations, but they also possessed a burgeoning knowledge of astrology. This forerunner of modern astronomy held the key to many problems, including such diverse endeavors as healing the sick, counseling the king, or simply winning a battle. Of course, where there is astronomy, there must also be mathematics, crude or refined. To be sure, all the sciences, if one can call them by such a modern term, were the bedfellows of religion.

One cannot say of these strange bedfellows that one was bad and the other was good, that one was right and the other was wrong, or even that one dealt with the possible and the other with the impossible. They were so interlinked, so interdependent in those ancient days, that one could not exist without the other. One could even say that it was the ideal situation: science and religion cooperating with each other in mutual respect and dependency. In many ways it is a model for us in our day, despite the inadequacies and superstitions that governed the ancient system. It was an ideal arrangement because it consisted of a natural bringing together of separate interests.

What, then, happened to divide them? What caused the separation just short of outright divorce?

GROUNDS FOR DIVORCE?

In one sense there has been no permanent separation. If science and religion were truly divorced, there would be no communication at all between these two seemingly disparate views of reality. Yet there continues an argument that never dies, never isolates one from the other, because at the heart of the matter there is a *desire* for reconciliation. That's because there is an intuitive sense that the two views relate to a single cosmic reality.

Of course, there are individuals on both sides of the argument who do not appreciate the nature of the dialectic. By "dialectic" I am indicating a conflict between two opposing forces (science and religion, in this case). Rather than one side losing and the other winning, both sides grow and mature in a new and more mature appreciation of reality. By contrast, the die-hard materialist and the fundamentalist believer face each other across an unbridgeable gap. This unfortunate mental breach governs their lives as well as their respective views of history. It is a distorted, self-defeating, and grossly limited view because each group denies, from its own perspective, an entire dimension of reality.

When science and religion do finally converge, it will be a joyful thing to behold. Unlike the ancient union, governed primarily by ignorance and superstition, the new union will indissolubly combine the best of the two perceptions into one true reality. This momentous union will continue until the last day. It *will* be the last day, eschatologically speaking, because the strategy of God will have fulfilled the sacred dreams of humankind. It will be the religion/science dialectic that brings us to that final goal. It will be a rancorous, mostly painful process that forces our limited minds to increasing self-examination, ultimately bringing us to the realization of what it means to be authentically human.

Thus, the outlook of humankind is not totally polarized into two separate camps, scientific and religious. True, what was once a highly unified, almost inseparable marriage between science and religion in ancient times is now in disarray. We have stumbled, but not yet fallen. At this moment the dialectic is serving its purposes, carrying us along the painful road to *becoming* what we were meant to be. In the words of T. S. Eliot ("Little Gidding," *Four Quartets*):

We will not cease from exploration
And the end of all our exploring
Will be to arrive where we started
And know the place for the first time.

We will know the place for the first time because the marriage of science and religion will be made in heaven and perfected in the crucible of time. The old union was fraught with suspicion and mistrust, ignorance and superstition, cunning and magic. In that system, there was no space for authentic living, no room for true love, no comfortable bed for the two partners to lie upon. In those circumstances, the separation was inevitable.

The marriage did not fall apart all at once. It was a gradual thing. In ancient Babylon, the priests were also the judges, the lawyers, and the physicians, a logical arrangement in those times because the law and medicine, like theology, were of divine origin. The Babylonians as well as the Assyrians (the ancient power that overran the Northern Kingdom of Israel in 721 BC) differentiated their demons in a similar manner as we do our germs. There was a demon for wasting diseases, for liver troubles, for women's diseases, and so on, so that every sick person was possessed by a different kind of demon.

One of the first indications of a separation is described by Herodotus while in Babylon (Book 1 of *The History*, trans. Rawlinson). The ancient historian tells of the sick being brought out into the marketplace. Herodotus does not mention the priestly physician as he describes the activity in the Babylonian marketplace.

> ...when a man is ill, they lay him in the public square, and the passers-by come up to him, and if they have ever had his disease themselves or have known of any one who has suffered from it, they give him advice, recommending him to do whatever they found good in their own case, or in the case known to them; and no one is allowed to pass the sick man in silence without asking him what his ailment is.

There was no consulting with a priest here; the ill person placed faith in the advice of a neighbor or friend. In a sense, this constituted the practice of medicine outside the purview of the religious leader.

In ancient Babylon the first physicians (other than a priestly physician) were the sick person's neighbors. In addition, there was a sharp distinction between surgeons and physicians. Apparently there were rules and restrictions that applied to the surgeons (physicians who were *not* priests) that did not affect the physicians (who *were* priests). According to Ralph Major (*The History of Medicine,* 27) such laws were written half a millennium before the time of Moses:

> If a physician operates on a man for a severe wound with a bronze lancet and cause the man's death; or open an abscess [in the eye] of a man with a bronze lancet and destroy the man's eye they shall cut off his fingers.
>
> If a physician operates on a slave of a freeman with a bronze lancet and cause his death, he shall restore a slave of equal value.

Other restrictions describe the fees that a physician is to receive following a successful surgical procedure. According to Major, there is little mention made of restrictions as they might apply to the practice of medicine, which, unlike surgery, was an activity under the aegis of the priests.

A MARRIAGE OF MYTHIC ORIGINS

The origins of both science and religion are shrouded in myth, yet we know that religion made use of instructive applications of myth. Some of the most sophisticated and elusive truths of religion are contained in the wonderful stories of the Bible, and in the epic tales inscribed on clay tablets originating with the early Mesopotamian civilizations. Modern science does not capitalize on its own mythic beginnings in the same light. If anything, most modern scientists, unlike their theological counterparts, are totally unaware of the primordial origins of their discipline. Further, modern science tends to impugn its mythic origins precisely because of its close ties to the early religions.

Ancient Egyptian medicine, for example, began with its priests, but it came to be closely associated with the name of Imhotep, who was deified sometime after his death. According to some traditions he was also an architect, priest, astronomer, magician, and sage, all this in addition to his role as a physician. About a century after his death (c. 2850 BC), Imhotep was considered a demigod; much later, writes Major, he was elevated to the status of a god. As the worship of Imhotep spread into lower Egypt, he became the god of medicine. The ancient Greeks came to identify him with their own god of medicine, Asclepios. Major says the Egyptian physician, as an inherently religious person, would call on his gods to assist his efforts at healing the patient.

The practice of calling on a deity for assistance in healing the sick is denigrated by some modern thinkers who label it "magical formulae or incantations," according to Fielding Garrison. To them it seems, at bottom, no different from a Christian physician in the twentieth century praying for divine assistance. In both instances, the ancient and the modern, the physician is operating from the perspective of faith in a higher power. Garrison goes so far as to say, "wherever this frame of mind persists, there is no possibility of advancement for medicine" (*History of Medicine*, 18).

Garrison's remark may be as shortsighted as it is judgmental. One cannot read an ancient text as though it were completely and unalterably dead, along with the human that wrote it. To do so would be to assume that the text itself tells us nothing about the human creature, ancient or modern, that is helpful even in a historical-critical sense. Such views can only poison useful research into the treasures of the past. Certainly, the logic of science and modern experimentation, as important as they are to medical advances, should not be used to dismiss, out of hand, the "incantations" of the past. One must be careful about any absolute measuring stick of his or her own conception, especially if it is used to canonize the present system.

Philo, a diasporic Jew who lived in Alexandria at the time of Christ, recognized the human failings of the physician very well. What he says is a lesson in humility for all who look to modern scientific skills as the final answer to the ills of humankind:

> For, as in medicine some practitioners who know how to cure almost every complaint, and disease, and infirmity,

can nevertheless give no true or even probable account of any one of them; and on the other hand, others are very clever, as far as giving an account of the diseases goes, and in explaining their symptoms and causes, and other modes of cure, and are the most excellent interpreters possible of the principles of which their art is made up, but are utterly useless in the matter of attending the bodies of the sick, to the cure of which they are not able to contribute even the slightest assistance. In the same way, those who have devoted themselves to practical wisdom have often neglected to pay attention to their language; and those who have learnt their professions thoroughly as far as words go, have yet treasured up no good instruction in their soul. (*The Works of Philo*, 116)

It can be said that we are divided today in much the same way into those who are blessed with great practical skills and those who are the technical experts of the world. Should the ones with the technical skills refuse to seek out the advice of those who are the most helpful in practical living? If so, our species may be prescribing a formula for disaster. Both science and religion should take note of Philo's important observation.

Prayer and the practice of medicine should go hand in hand. *Time* magazine devoted a cover story to this topic (June 24, 1996). A 1995 study at Dartmouth-Hitchcock Medical Center revealed that one of the best predictors of successful heart surgery was the degree to which patients drew comfort from their religious faith. Numerous studies, reports *Time*, show data that reveal a lower rate of depression and of anxiety-related illness among the religiously committed. Indeed, medicine and spirituality, a mixture that used to spell professional suicide to the physician, is now becoming an accepted practice, if not a common one. There is evidence here of a flirtation going on between science and religion. The dialectic continues, but the marriage bed is, as yet, unoccupied. The two parties have begun a limited intimacy once more, but they are suspicious still, and there is a reluctance to dance to the ancient melody.

SCIENCE, FAITH AND THE HIDDEN GOD

God does not sit visibly on a mountain top directing humanity's every move, punishing his creatures when they are disobedient, and rewarding them when they fear and love him. Indeed, if God were this evident to us, there would be no reason for faith. God would not be invisible or hidden from his human creatures.

The concept of an invisible God is an important link to a full appreciation, if such is possible, of the Christian landscape. Let us imagine a visible *(unhidden)* deity of a certain hypothetical world. This God watches the every move of his subjects from on high, and he holds a big stick in his right hand (metaphorically speaking), ready to swat anyone who disobeys his divine will. The people of this hypothetical world would be thinking, self-reflecting individuals, just like us, and so every man, woman, and child who lived in this world would be very good because no one goes looking to be wiped out by their God. It may not be a bad place in which to live if the inhabitants didn't mind the absence of freedom. Still, it may be possible that a God like this would not inhibit freedom entirely. Some daring individuals might be willing to get swatted if for no other reason than to allay the boredom of being good all the time.

But even if such a visible God did not totally obliterate freedom, it would certainly be curtailed. There would be little call for loving such a deity, only fearing him. One thing such a God would totally obliterate, however, is *faith*. One cannot have faith in the existence of a God that is so manifestly present. There would not be much room for hope, either, especially if this God were the all-powerful despot depicted here.

The above scenario may be regarded as one explanation for the real God of the universe remaining invisible, and for the importance of faith. Practically speaking, if such can be said of God's motives, he remains hidden from sight for two good reasons. First, because he does not want to obliterate the all-important elements of worship, namely faith and hope; and second, because God is so utterly incomprehensible to us at humankind's present stage of development. The real God of the universe must therefore remain for us, as expressed in the title of an anonymous work from the fourteenth century, hidden behind *The Cloud of Unknowing*. We can only partially know God by

71

exaggerating the best of human attributes to an infinite degree. The real God of the universe, I believe, remains invisible because humanity is not ready for, and would be totally blinded by, any face-to-face encounter.

Absolute certainty of God's existence, if such were possible before the end of time, would stifle, if not extinguish, *spiritual growth*. Humankind would no longer seek the face of God because the object of such seeking would be known already. All quests after knowledge, including the sciences, would be utterly constrained. Who would want to dabble in such mundane pursuits as studying molecular genetics or developing better rocket fuels when it is possible to bask in the glory of a loving God? Ironically, it may seem, faith ultimately becomes just as important to science as it does to religion.

Faith in God, the Supreme Intelligence behind creation, is therefore important to science as well as the faithful Christian, Jew, or Muslim. For some reason not totally known or understood to us in the present, God wants his human creatures—entangled in the perils of human sinfulness and human enterprise, existing and subsisting within the created universe with all its laws of science and nature— to find their own way to a higher level of existence. Then and only then will God be fully revealed to us. Evidence for this conclusion comes by way of our God-given curiosity and thirst for knowledge. This penchant contains an inborn goal, one that God sees in the distant future of humanity. Human religion can bring us to merely a vague awareness of this goal or the consequences of reaching it, but it is one that is nevertheless exciting. Intrinsic to our very *Being*, as the philosophers tell us, is *becoming*. Unless humankind is becoming something greater than it already is, then creation makes no sense at all. If all one can do is sit passively and await the tooting of horns and the coming of Christ from heaven on a cloud, then he or she is missing the most exciting of gifts from God. These gifts include the reality of a world in the process of innovation, the struggle for authenticity in life, and the daily renaissance of discovery and personal growth in the created universe. The world is evolving just as is the human species, and it is not helpful to us to suppress this obvious reality.

When one looks at science and religion in this context, it is easy to see how these two approaches to reality are natural partners in a long evolutionary journey. For all the reasons given above, faith is important, even indispensable, to both endeavors. What an irony and what a shock to the ego this might seem to those who worship science as the only truth. The proponents of godless evolution would never accept this conclusion, of course, unless they were the recipients of a direct revelation from God, much as the apostle Paul experienced on the road to Damascus. This great truth will come in God's own time, I am convinced, because the ongoing dialectic between science and religion is leading all humanity in the direction of union in the one glorious reality. One day the reciprocal dependencies of science and religion will become so overwhelming that only the hardened atheist will be able to resist. In those blessed days, everyone will see themselves, perhaps for the first time, as truly created in the image of God.

Over and again we see the same pattern, that of a tendency toward unity. It is the greatest enterprise of religion as well as science. Theoretical physicists are struggling with the formulation of a unified "theory of everything." Such a formulation would explain the physical universe from the smallest "string" to the largest cluster of galaxies. The observations of biological and intellectual convergence in humankind cannot be denied.

It is such patterns of behavior in the realms of science and religion that point to the idea of a transcendent being, a spiritual goal to be achieved using the tools at hand. Strangely, it may seem, we are moving from the complex to the simple. Whether it be one theory that describes the laws of all the material universe, or one grand appreciation for the magnificent God of creation, we seem to be headed in the right direction. God may be physically hidden from us, but he waits to be found within the mysteries of creation. God does not want to be a tree falling in a dead wilderness.

THE PSYCHOLOGY OF BELIEF

> But it is a fact that, in addition to memories from a long-distant past, completely new thoughts and creative ideas can also present themselves from the unconscious—thoughts and ideas that have never been conscious before.
>
> —C. G. Jung, *Man and His Symbols*

An article in *Time* magazine asks the question, "Which came first, God, or the need for God?" In other words, is there such a thing as a "God gene"? The article is based on a book by molecular biologist Dean Hamer (*The God Gene: How Faith Is Hardwired in Our Genes*). Hamer proclaims (presumably based on his research), "I think we [humans] follow the basic law of nature, which is that we're a bunch of chemical reactions running around in a bag." The hypothesis in itself is an over-simplification. Provided that the chemical makeup of the brain has some elements one could identify as "spiritually coded," there would still be a large number of factors involved (Hamer, guoted in Jeffrey Kluger et al., "Is God in Our Genes?" *Time* magazine, August 5, 2004, 64 and 65).

Undoubtedly, *something* is going on in the human brain that predisposes most of us to spiritual urgings. Explaining the spiritual appetite, however, cannot explain it out of existence. It is the same as in the conversion experience of the apostle Paul. Did a truly miraculous event cause the apostle's conversion, or did Paul experience a temporal lobe seizure? In the final analysis, it does not matter which is true. Paul went on to become "the lion of God."

It is one thing to say that the human brain has a built-in spirituality and another to conclude that God is an artifact of the brain. Mindless statements such as these seem to flow easily from the mouths of those who are comfortable in their atheism. I am more concerned here with the psychology of belief than the chemistry of belief. Most of us can agree that the tendency toward belief in some kind of transcendent being is universal among the peoples of the world, whether modern or primitive.

The scientist is moved by curiosity, the need to *know*, an impulse that is instinctive in our species. One might ask, "Is there also an instinctive need for religion deep in our psychic makeup?" To answer this question, psychologists have attempted to probe the human psyche as it exists *before normal sensory input.*

PSYCHOLOGY AND RELIGIOSITY

The tabula rasa, or "clean slate," is the mind as it exists before it receives the impressions and influences gained from experience. To explore behind the tabula rasa is one of the special tasks of present-day psychology, as it attempts to better understand if there is an innate source of human religiosity. It is inference, rather than any measurement scheme, that can take us behind the sensory facade, which can span the full compass of the human psyche. According to Thorne Shipley (*Classics in Psychology*), it is through the insights of Gestalt psychologists that logic, perception, ethics, and aesthetics are all seen to be founded upon origins lying well in back of that mentally clean slate. This is *the* precise starting point of C. G. Jung's search for what he termed "archetypes," that is, the inherited predispositions that lie behind the tabula rasa and are inherited rather than learned.

In the important area of humankind's compelling religiosity, much of the recent movements in psychology have remained silent, says Shipley. The two greatest voids in the psychology of Freud, for example, were religion and ethics. In both areas, more is owed to anthropology than to psychology. Freud, asserts Shipley, understood neither religion nor ethics, and claimed to find no place for religious experiences in his own life. And yet the most serious intellectual upheaval that Freud experienced—his break with C. G. Jung—was basically over this issue. In the religious aspect of the human psyche, Jung touched elements of our unconscious that Freud did not.

The areas of religion and ethics constitute the most important challenge to psychology today. There are elements of the human condition on both sides of the tabula rasa, the sensory and presensory, that should eventually blend into a more healthy and complete description of the human personality. But no one, to this point, has been able to do so. To provide some inkling of how things stand today, it seems appropriate to examine and contrast two of the most important pioneers in the field of clinical psychology and psychoanalysis, Sigmund Freud and Carl Gustav Jung.

Sigmund Freud (1856–1939)

Freud was a Viennese psychoanalyst who lived a rather quiet life in academia and who also had a private clinical practice. He was forced to leave Vienna by the Nazis and moved to London, where he lived and eventually died. His most seminal work, *The Interpretation of Dreams,* was published in 1900.

Freud's system was void of any God, and rather than speculate about materialism, idealism, or creation itself, he chose to study the human psyche as the royal road to reality. The inner life, according to Freud, is mysterious as well as multilayered, while the conscious life is just the tip of an iceberg. The human psyche is something like a vast, uncharted continent, believed Freud, which includes three regions: the *id,* the instinctual drives seeking immediate gratification; the *ego,* a kind of primitive conscience, limiting the id for the purpose of the life and health of the organism; and the *superego,* a more developed conscience formed by society's influence, limiting the id for the purpose of both individual and societal survival. These inner forces are in constant turmoil, struggling one against the other. In this, at least, Freud joined with Hegel, Marx, and Darwin in sensing reality as dynamic and tumultuous. The basic questions were how to cope with such conflict, and how to react to it.

The main problem with humanity, as Freud perceived it, is that many people are caught up in a condition of *repression;* that is, a pushing of unpleasant memories or disagreeable ideas from the conscious mind into the unconscious, with the consequence of poor adjustment to the conflicts of the inner self. This happens when one is faced with the primal human drives of nourishment, sex, and security, or such emotions as fear, anger, and love. The individual soon learns, usually through painful experience, that these appetites cannot be immediately or completely gratified. Denial or repression of these inner conflicts results in their surfacing in some form, mostly neurotic, or in some kind of unusual activity. A severe repression may result in psychosis, a partial or complete splitting of the individual's consciousness from reality.

Freud is probably best known as the man who tried to break down sexual inhibitions. This is partly true. A child of the Victorian Age, Freud was all too aware of the obsession with sexuality, often from the puritanical or fearful point of view that was part of that age. Freud's pioneering development of psychoanalysis sought to remedy these obsessions. In pursuit of the unconscious mind, he endeavored to probe the individual's heart of darkness, the inner jungle as it were. Thus, through dreams, free-association, hypnosis, and the now-famous Freudian slips, one could find the realities behind the surface of consciousness. Once these were laid bare, the individual, with the help of the therapist, could devise ways of coming to grips with the real problem. Later, followers of Freud would disagree with some of his conclusions, without discounting his major contributions to the field. C. G. Jung was one of these followers who eventually broke with Freud on the fundamental issue of the ultimate meaning of religiosity as manifested in the human psyche.

> Sigmund Freud also was an active opponent of the traditional religious perspective....Religion, Freud considered, is a human construct, a psychological projection of the lost father figure. We invent a father-god in order to feel more secure and at home in an alien, indifferent, even hostile universe....If humanity is to become more healthy psychologically, religion had to go....
>
> What were the responses of thoughtful theologians in the wake of Freud's very serious theological challenge?
>
> 1. They pointed out that the God of the Western religions—Judaism, Christianity, Islam—provided not just comfort in the lives of believers, but challenge and *in*security. Nowhere was this more apparent than in the fulminations of the Hebrew prophets. [Freud did not seem to understand this balance.]

77

2. They pointed out that Freud's own argument had an assumption lurking beneath it: that *because* humanity longs desperately for something or someone, it *must* therefore be nonexistent. And where [these critics asked] was the scientific warrant for that position? They thus inverted Freud's own analysis to suggest (as did Jung in part) that a drive so profoundly rooted in the human psyche could well point to a cosmic reality not only printed into the psychic structure, but existing beyond it as well. (Crews, *The Ultimate Questions*, 76)

Carl Gustav Jung (1875–1961)

From 1906 to 1913, C. G. Jung was one of the most enthusiastic adherents and disciples of Sigmund Freud. Jung began his professional career as a clinical psychiatrist, but at the same time he showed a great deal of interest in the spiritual yearnings of humankind, which he believed were fundamental to the psyche. As a psychologist and a psychotherapist, he perceived the goal of his work to be that of a healer of the psyche. He made pointed reference to the great religions of the world, which had ministered to the human psyche and provided guidelines for the "development of the soul." Almost all of his writings concerned the problems that an individual encounters in the course of his or her psychic development, and, ultimately, with the *meaning of life* itself. According to Wallace B. Clift (Preface to his *Jung and Christianity*), Jung said, "Man cannot stand a meaningless life." Jung made this statement during his 1959 BBC interview given shortly before his death.

In Jung's view of the psyche, as in Freud's, there is a conscious and an unconscious. Access to the unconscious must of necessity be approached through the conscious psyche. The ego is at the center of consciousness and is the awareness of the self *as* self. In examining the unconscious, Jung made a distinction between the "personal unconscious" and the "collective unconscious" (the latter also called the "impersonal" or "superpersonal unconscious"). The *personal* unconscious consists of forgotten, repressed, or subliminally (subconsciously) perceived things of every kind that can be related to the life experiences of the individual. By contrast, the *collective* unconscious contains the whole spiritual heritage of humankind's evolution, embedded somehow in the genetic makeup of every individual. It consists of elements characteristic of the human species, born anew as it were, in the brain structure of every individual.

The conscious mind develops over the lifetime of the individual. It succeeds in bringing about the necessary adaptations and adjustments to the environment or to the conscious world. Aspects of conscious experience may be forgotten or repressed and thereby become a part of the personal unconscious. The content of this personal unconscious, especially those elements that have been repressed, were regarded by Freud as one of the root mechanisms in evoking a neurosis.

Here one should distinguish between *suppression* and *repression*. Suppression amounts to a conscious moral choice, says Jung, but repression is an "immoral penchant" for getting rid of disagreeable decisions (*Psychology and Religion*, 91). Experiences that are suppressed may lead to worry, conflict, and suffering, but never cause the typical patterns of a neurosis, as does repression.

Neurosis, asserts Jung, is a substitute for legitimate suffering. We have certain ideas as to how a civilized or moral individual should live, and we occasionally do our best to fulfill these ambitions and expectations. But as nature has not bestowed the same blessings upon each of her children, some of them are more gifted than others in regard to the functioning of the psyche. Thus, there are people who can just barely afford to live properly and respectably. Their sins are either minor, or they manage to conceal them from their conscious minds. One may tend to be lenient with sinners who are not conscious of their sins, but nature is not at all lenient with unconscious sinners. She punishes them just as severely as if they had committed a conscious offense. Everyone carries a shadow lurking beneath the conscious mind, believes Jung, "and the less it is embodied in the individual's conscious life, the blacker and denser it is" (ibid.).

We carry our past with us, that is, the primitive and inferior person with all the desires and emotions that these imply. It is only by a considerable effort that we can detach ourselves from this burden. In the case of a neurosis, if one wants to be healed, it is necessary for the person's conscious personality and his shadow to learn to live together (*Psychology and Religion*, 93).

The collective unconscious is said *not to be derivative of personal experience.* It is, rather, the source of the instinctual forces of the psyche and of the categories that regulate them, namely, the *archetypes.* Jung made use of the term *archetype* to refer to the contents of the collective unconscious. The archetypes are analogous to the instincts, except that the instincts have their effects on the body, whereas the archetypes operate in the psyche. Jung explains that what we properly call instincts are physiological urges and are perceived by the senses as such. At the same time instincts may also manifest themselves in fantasies and often reveal themselves in symbolic images. These manifestations are what Jung calls archetypes. Archetypes, then, are an instinctive *trend,* such as the impulse of birds to build nests, or ants to form organized colonies. In this regard Jung relates the following:

> I vividly recall the case of a professor who had a sudden vision and thought he was insane. He came to see me in a state of complete panic. I simply took a 400-year-old book from the shelf and showed him an old woodcut depicting his very vision. "There's no reason for you to believe you are insane," I told him. "They knew about your vision 400 years ago." Whereupon he sat down entirely deflated, but once more normal. (*Man and His Symbols,* 58)

Jung has been roundly criticized for his modern gnosticism in a scholarly work by Maurice Friedman (*Religion and Psychology,* 91). According to Friedman, Jung has placed the collective psyche, or self, as his touchstone of reality. In this scenario the inner God would be the only God. This inevitably leads to the psychology of Jung becoming the only admissible metaphysic, while remaining for Jung himself "an empirical science." The question Friedman asks is, can it be both at once?

This criticism might also apply to the best-selling novel *The Celestine Prophecy* by James Redfield. But for the commercial flavor of the novel and its companion publication, *Experiential Guide* by Redfield and Carol Adrienne, this book would have remained a simple novel about an extraordinary, but purely fictional, spiritual experience. It is now evident, however, that the author(s) intend much more, with study guides, the formation of study groups, and so on, all indicating that the "nine insights" (in Redfields's mind) *go far beyond mere* fiction. To me, Redfield's effort is little more than warmed-over gnosticism, in which a special kind of knowledge (from the Greek *gnosis,* which means "knowledge") gets you a ticket to eternal life. Emphasis on the idea of pure spirit living outside the body, thereby escaping the constraints of worldly existence, also suggests gnostic ideas.

Redfield's book does point to a deep hunger for spiritual experience, at least among the American public. To the extent that it has drawn more individuals to consider the spiritual aspects of reality more seriously, I compliment the author. My fear is that those who look for religious experiences through the contemplation of Redfield's nine insights might be disillusioned and thus discouraged from other, more time-tested ways of prayer and meditation.

As I have indicated, Jungian psychology has been cited as one of the legitimizing backgrounds of Redfield's nine insights. All criticism aside, however, Jung has made an enormous contribution to religious thinking; his discovery of distinctly religious elements within the unconscious, for example, is certainly an insight worthy of further thought and scholarly investigation. Where Friedman believes Jung made an error is in the divinization of the unconscious insofar as this concept evokes belief in a psychologized God (Friedman, 92).

It is certainly not farfetched that the Jungian view suggests a kind of modern gnosticism, and that Jung immerses early Christian practices into the somewhat nebulous realm of psychology and psychoanalysis. A distinction here must be made, however, between the view of the Christian mystics—such as Teresa of Avila, John of the Cross, Julian of Norwich—and others who also seek the God within, and the gnostic view. We are "God's temple and God's Spirit dwells in you," says the apostle Paul (1 Cor 3:16), an article of faith that can be ascribed to all practicing Christians. The difference lies in the gnostic view that says the God within, the *immanent God,* is the *only God;* that is, the *Wholly Other,* or *transcendent, God* of Hebrew-Christian tradition does not exist. The secret of gnosis, as Elaine Pagels puts it, is "to know oneself, at the deepest level, [which] is simultaneously to know God" (Pagels, *The Gnostic Gospels,* xix). One should hasten to add, however, that this does not mean that modern Christians, or the Christian mystics, believe in two Gods. Rather, the God of *imma-*

nence and the God of *transcendence* are the same one God who abides in us *immanently* while at the same moment *transcends* the space-time constraints to which all of us beings of the flesh are bound.

As I have attempted to make evident, the Hebraic heart of the Old Testament has all the perceived properties of the Jungian psyche, and much more (Shackleford, *The Biblical Heart*). When understood in its fullest anthropological sense, the biblical heart brings us closer to an understanding of God's relationship to his human creatures, and vice versa, than does any strictly Jungian approach to religion. The Jungian psyche, I hasten to add, is certainly an important impetus toward a better understanding of the deeper mysteries of the Hebraic (biblical) heart.

8

SCIENCE AND THE QUESTION OF REALITY

> But what is significant in psychic life is always below the horizon of consciousness, and when we speak of the spiritual problems of modern man we are dealing with things that are barely visible—with the most intimate and fragile things—with flowers that open only in the night.
> —C. G. Jung, *Modern Man in Search of a Soul*

Their fascination with each other when they were newly married has faded from memory. They have forgotten they were ever in love. It was such a beautiful relationship, the two of them working hand in hand for the people: the one tending to their spiritual needs, the other involved in more practical matters, such as when to plant crops and how to irrigate them in the dry season.

She (*science*) loved to examine flowers, heal the sick with her collection of herbs, and study those myriad pinpoints of light in the heavens, the stars. She loved to watch their movements, to see if they came back to the same location with each cycle of nature. Most of all, she was fascinated with those mysterious emanations, mostly brighter than the other lights, that seemed to have a will of their own, moving mysteriously, not at all like the stars.

He (*religion*) explained to her that those bodies of light that moved independently are the gods. "If you watch them carefully, you can understand what they are saying, and warn the king of an impending disaster, or foretell some great and momentous favor. For the most part," he said, "these gods are unpredictable, like their motions in the sky. That is why we must never incur their anger and always make proper sacrifices to them. Sometimes, though, even when we do everything right, they still become angry. They flood the fields and ruin the crops. The people starve. Other times they cause the earth itself to shake, and the mountains to belch flames, throwing rocks high into the air and killing many people. I wish I knew better how to deal with these gods," he told her, "then I could serve the people better."

"I will help you," she told him, enthusiastically. "There must be some things these gods do over and over, some consistency in their movements across the sky at different times and in different seasons. We will work together, you and I, and as partners we can serve king and people better."

And so the young couple frolicked together in the grassy hillside, delighting in each other's stories, exploring their youthful bodies, confessing their undying love. It was, indeed, a union made in heaven. Then one day he overheard her speaking with the king, telling him things that were not so, even things about the gods that could not be true. Worst of all she told the king that he, her beloved, was wrong about a lot of things, that he kept his head in the clouds, that he did not see things as they really are, that he even made things up.

The king was furious with *science* and threw her out of his chambers. What would become of their world, thought the king, if all those things they had believed from the beginning, passed down by the ancient fathers, were to come to naught? No, it could not be, and he would not hear of it.

And so *religion* became the real power in the land, while *science* sulked. It came to pass that *science* and *religion* no longer frolicked in the grass, no longer explored one another's bodies. In fact, they were not even on speaking terms. There were attempts at reconciliation, but both had the same ambition: to be first in line to the king, to be the power that had the king's ear. Somehow they had forgotten how they used to work together, to advise one another in mutual respect. As time went on, it seemed as if there never had been any love between them.

This little fantasy gets at the split between science and religion in the early history of their relationship. The historical separation was more complex than this simple fantasy reveals because science and magic and religion were all mixed together in the minds of the people. Certainly, science and religion, as it existed among ancient civilizations, was not as well-developed a concept as it is today.

RELIGION AND ASTRONOMY

Astronomy is a very ancient science, although, in view of its religious and magical connections, it is usually described under the rubric of astrology. In spite of these connections, the Babylonians and the Egyptians made fairly accurate astronomical observations. These observations had some practical applications, as well as some superstitious ones. In Babylon the movements of the sun, moon, stars, and planets, all godly manifestations, were somehow related to, or presaged, events to occur. The knowledge and accuracy of Babylonian astrologer-priests regarding the celestial system was astounding. Astrology in Babylon was devoted primarily to affairs of state (e.g., to determine the outcome of military expeditions). It was also used to ascertain the course and outcome of disease and to foretell good and bad agricultural years. As to the astronomical expertise of ancient Egypt, Herodotus reports the following:

> The Egyptians, they said, were the first to discover the solar year, and to portion out its course into twelve parts. They obtained this knowledge from the stars. To my mind they contrive their year much more cleverly than the Greeks, for these last[,] every other year[,] intercalate a whole month, but the Egyptians, dividing the year into twelve months of thirty days each, add every year a space of five days besides, whereby the circuit of seasons is made to return with uniformity. (*The History,* Book 1)

The Babylonians have long been regarded as especially proficient in mathematics and astronomy. They also made accurate records of many celestial events. During the reign of Nebuchadnezzar (the Babylonian king who destroyed Jerusalem in 587 BC), they plotted the orbits of the sun and moon, recorded the eclipses, calculated the courses of planets, distinguished between planets and stars, determined the solstices and equinoxes, and further divided the measurement of the degree into sixty minutes. Again, it was the priests and the religion of the Babylonians that set the stage for all these discoveries. Astronomy (astrology) and mathematics were perhaps more closely related to the ancient religions of the world than even medicine, in

85

light of the various forms the medical arts took. Babylonian surgeons, as mentioned earlier, may not have been associated with the priestly elite at all.

Religion continued to be closely aligned with astronomy for many centuries. The conclusions of Ptolemy, the Egyptian astronomer, came to be regarded as inviolable by the early Christian Church. Ptolemy made such an impression on future generations that men would endanger their lives for daring to question his cosmic system and basic assumptions. His fame is owed to a workable system, erroneous as it was, to explain the relationships of the stars and planets. Ptolemy's insistence on the absolute immobility of the Earth and its position as the center of the universe proved to be strongly attractive to the church and its theologians, since it provided astronomical evidence for the dignity of the human race. That is, if the Earth were at the center of the universe, it was one more proof of the special position and high regard of God for humankind.

All this fanciful thinking, as attractive as it may have been, came to an end with the revolution set in motion by Copernicus. His observations were a crucial milestone and perhaps symbolic of the transition from the medieval to the modern worlds. Indeed, the works of Copernicus set in motion the achievements of Galileo, Kepler, and Newton, which completed the overthrow of the medieval world view. Let's look at two of these influential men.

Copernicus (1473–1543)

Niklas Koppernigk (more commonly known by his Latin name, *Copernicus*) was born in Torun in Poland and educated in Cracow, Bologna, Ferrara, and Padua. A splendid example of the medieval scholar, his genius was almost universal, and his reading ranged from economics and medicine to mathematics and astronomy. He was greatly influenced by one of his instructors, Domenico Novaro, who had criticized the complexities of the Ptolemaic system. Copernicus was thus encouraged to take up the study of the classics so as to discover the objections to the concept that Earth was fixed and immovable and at the center of the universe. He found that there were great thinkers of antiquity, such as the Greek astronomer Aristarchus of

Samos (third century BC), who taught that Earth rotated on its own axis, and that the sun was the center of an immeasurably great universe.

Copernicus's alternative to Ptolemaic astronomy took many years of preparation, and his conclusions were reached largely by the use of mathematics, logic, and observation. He went about setting the heavenly bodies in relation to the sun at the center (heliocentric theory) and considering Earth as one of the sun's planets. In doing so Copernicus found that he could account for most heavenly movements. He demonstrated the rotation of Earth on its axis, as well as its movement around the sun. His system greatly simplified that of Ptolemy and explained more. His definitive work, *De Revolutionibus Orbium Caelestium,* was published shortly before he died. A preface to the book was later found to have been written by a Lutheran minister named Osiander, intending to placate the Protestants by describing the work as a "mathematical exercise" (Schwartz and Bishop, *Moments of Discovery,* 219). This preface may have been the reason the Copernican ideas failed to have an immediate revolutionary effect. The Copernican model and the Ptolemaic system were taught as alternative explanations until the eighteenth century, even at Harvard and Yale.

Galileo

Another great astronomer, Galileo Galilei (1564–1642), was born at Pisa, Italy, and educated in a monastery, as was the custom for a nobleman's son. He is known for many insights, in addition to his contributions to astronomy, but it was astronomy that brought him the most fame. He pondered the Copernican model with the aid of his new instrument, the telescope. The original telescope was developed in the Netherlands, but Galileo's improvements greatly increased its magnifying power. With his telescope he observed protuberances on the sun, the mountains of the moon, and the innumerable stars that composed the Milky Way. His descriptions of these discoveries, particularly the enunciation of his Copernican views, brought about his conflict with the church. For the first time the full impact of the revolutionary ideas of Copernicus, now substantiated by Galileo, were having an effect on the church's religious teaching. Galileo was reprimanded but allowed to continue his studies provided that he treated the Copernican thesis of daily revolution of the Earth not as an absolute truth, but as a hypothesis to facilitate mathematical calculations. He continued to work unmolested for another nineteen years until 1632, when he published his *Dialogue on the Two Chief Systems of the World*. The church leaders were displeased because the work was published in Italian (instead of Latin) and was therefore available to any ordinary citizen who could read. Galileo and the whole Copernican doctrine were condemned, and the astronomer was once again brought before the Inquisition. He was compelled to sign a recognition of the church's authority in these matters. Although Galileo kept himself out of controversy from this time on, others did not.

It is not my purpose here to go into the entire history of the conflict between science and religion. What I do want to bring out, however, is that many still point to the Galileo episode as if it happened yesterday. It is used by the enemies of religion as though Christianity, the Catholic Church in particular, has not matured since the days when Galileo was alive. But one need only look at the ongoing dialectic between science and religion today to see the enormous progress that has been made. Indeed, the outlook of science, as well as that of religion, has become more open to new ideas and concepts. As pointed out earlier, the idea of biological evolution, once thought of as among the greatest enemies of religion, is now regarded by many Catholic scholars as a beautiful scenario from which to view the handiwork of God.

It may be that I have oversimplified the Hegelian dialectic, but the forces of history do seem to be working as the great philosopher of history predicted. Thus, as thesis is confronted by antithesis in the course of history, there is most always a new synthesis of ideas that result. The differences are not always solved democratically, or without attendant violence, but solutions do come about eventually and result in the growth and maturity of spiritual consciousness.

There will probably always be objections to evolution, among other scientific pronouncements, but there has been an enormous change in attitudes, just in my lifetime, certainly since the time of the Scopes "Monkey Trial" in 1924, in which a high school biology teacher was tried for teaching evolution. These changes are good for both science and religion. Among other things, scientific and religious arrogance has diminished considerably. For the most part, the two fields of endeavor are now talking to one another without rancor, and this has to be a good sign. There are problems in communication to overcome, however, some of which I will address in the pages to follow.

9

THE DEMONS OF RELIGION

Yet among the mature we do speak wisdom, though it is not a wisdom of this age or of the rulers of this age, who are doomed to perish. But we speak God's wisdom, secret and hidden, which God decreed before the ages for our glory. None of the rulers of this age understood this; for if they had, they would not have crucified the Lord of glory.

—1 Cor 2:6–8

In this chapter title, I am using *demons* as a metaphor for the prejudicial attitudes, perceptions, and forces keeping the natural partnership of science and religion at odds. It is a term from ancient times used to indicate a malady, or some deviation from the natural order of things; perhaps even a power, supernatural or magical, that had to be reckoned with. Now that humankind is more educated, we can at least identify the etiologic agent (bacteria, viruses, and so on) as the root cause of a number of pathologies known to exist in those ancient times.

Most of our modern diseases may well have been the "demons" of Babylonia, or of first-century Palestine, when Jesus of Nazareth lived. So what are our present-day demons? What are the sometimes-hidden, mostly unrecognized forces, of the twentieth century that keep science and religion apart? Are they just ignorance, pure and simple? Or are they just the slow evolution in human growth toward a more mature state of being? As I shall try to demonstrate, science and religion both have demons to reckon with. We will examine the demons of religion first.

There are many demons behind the religious pathologies we see on television and read about every day in the newspaper. These demons take several forms, infecting the powers of the intellect to a surprising degree. As such, they are a devastating insanity, and few, if any, seem to be totally immune to this infection. The first of these demons of religion are ones that unconsciously, certainly unintentionally, place limitations on the power of God.

DEMONS THAT LIMIT THE POWER AND FREEDOM OF GOD

In my opinion, this is a pervasive, yet difficult-to-recognize demon. It takes the form of placing limitations on the power (and freedom) of God. Why would any religious person, believing in an all-powerful and loving God, want to limit God's powers? What is the disease that brings this on? What are its symptoms?

Well, I suppose no religious person actually *wants* to limit God's powers, but it happens over and over again in the name of biblical integrity. We are told by literalist believers, for example, that God could not have created through the natural process of organic evolution. God had to create everything "just like the Book of Genesis tells us." Moreover, man and woman, created in the image of God, are a special creation (Gen 1) who lived in a state of innocence in the garden of Eden (Gen 2), all of which happened "just as the Bible says."

I can understand why some individuals and groups are protective of this literal "truth." I am even sympathetic with the fear and revulsion that results from attacks on the Bible that seem to undermine the integrity of the sacred text and, in so doing, devalue the basis of an entire system of beliefs. Once you allow flexibility in interpreting the biblical text, so the reasoning goes, where does one stop? If the story of Adam and Eve is not literally true, then where does one draw the line for the remainder of the Bible? Was there no such person as Moses, no Joshua, Samuel, or King David? Is the story of Jesus of Nazareth all a cruel fiction perpetrated against a gullible humanity?

I certainly understand these fears because I am coming from the same place as those who experience them. Most of us have moved through the Sunday-schoolish, childlike portrayals of biblical personages to a more mature appreciation of the great contributions of the inspired Hebrew writers and New Testament evangelists. As one grows in this appreciation, however, one comes to realize that some of the most feared changes and interpretations in the Bible have already come about. Ask any translator who has struggled with the ancient Hebrew language and tried to put the words into some semblance of a modern context, and you will see some of the difficulties: How would one put the literal translation into more understandable English, for example, of Moses' statement that he is of "uncircumcised lips" (Exod 6:12; RSV)? A similar difficulty for translation would be the exhortation in Deuteronomy (10:16; RSV) to "circumcise therefore the foreskin of your heart, and be no longer stiff-necked." In some of the more literal translations of the Bible, there is no attempt to render these examples more understandable. In others, however, Moses might be a "poor speaker" instead of having "uncircumcised lips."

The "uncircumcised heart," or the converse, the "circumcised heart," is packed with theological meaning that has to do with God's presence to us in history and the degree to which we are open to that presence. As a matter of fact, the word *heart,* whether in the original Hebrew of the Old Testament or in its Greek rendering in the New Testament, is the most frequently used anthropological term in the Bible. The *biblical heart,* to be sure, is a metaphor or symbol that accommodates some of the most sophisticated insights about the power, righteousness, and immanence of God. These important insights are frequently lost in translations that aim for clarity rather than accuracy. My own preferences in Bibles are the ones with the most literal translations of the ancient languages (Hebrew and Greek), accompanied by good study notes on each page to explain some of the more difficult passages.

Aside from translation difficulties, the cultural context of the ancient Israelite was so vastly different from ours, and that difference alone poses numerous problems, regardless of the accuracy of the modern presentation. Biblical scholars truly earn their bread in the difficult task of placing themselves within the ancient social context in order to better understand the intended meaning of the text. These types of investigations are commonly referred to as "historical criticism." It is a necessary step that must precede interpretations of the biblical text for you and me, the modern reader. Without historical criticism the ordinary devotee of the Bible will never appreciate the fullness and richness of the biblical text.

There are many, of course, who do not accept historical criticism in any shape, form, or fashion. They say that the reader, regardless of background or education, is the best interpreter of the Bible. This opinion, however, does not hold water because the Bible itself counsels us to get help in understanding its full meaning. The Ethiopian in Acts 8:30–31, struggling to understand the Book of Isaiah, is a good model of humility for all of us. Scriptural studies, like the specialties of medicine, are simply too diverse for any one person to master. Even the scholar, regardless of personal renown in the field, must depend on other scholars.

In a similar vein, the Second Letter of Peter (3:16) tells us that some things are hard to understand, and that the ignorant and unstable distort them to their own destruction; here he refers specifically to the writings of the apostle Paul, but his words apply as well to so many other passages that give rise to questions: What do Moses' uncircumcised lips have to do with us? For that matter, what does the exodus from Egypt over three-thousand years ago, or the wandering in the Sinai wilderness for forty years, have to do with twenty-first-century American Christians? Abraham and Moses rose to prominence out of a background of paganism. Was Abraham a pagan, then, who just happened to give *most* of his allegiance to the One God of the mountain, *El Shaddai*? Similarly, did all of the patriarchs of the Old Testament recognize multiple gods? When did true monotheism actually enter the biblical picture? These questions are raised not to confuse the reader. They are mentioned simply to illustrate some of the complicated issues that concern biblical scholars. Regardless of how one answers these questions, the closer we come to understanding those ancient times, the more we can appreciate the truth and sacredness of the Bible and read it as it should be read.

Scholars make the point that God is revealed within the prevailing social context of a particular historical time. Monotheism, therefore, did not just happen overnight. Rather it was allowed to evolve out of a pagan setting, gradually asserting itself as worshippers became more sophisticated, and as religious consciousness grew and matured. All of the great religions of the world are like this. Huston Smith (*The World's Religions*), a renowned authority on world religions and a devout Methodist, regards the relationship of Buddhism to Hinduism as similar to that of Christianity in its relationship to Judaism. Certainly there are parallels in the sense that the parent religions (Judaism and Hinduism) were limited to the domain of a particular

93

people and culture, while the offspring of these two ancient systems (Christianity and Buddhism) became more universal and transcultural in their appeal.

It makes sense that, if a given religion has its roots within the cultural setting of an ancient system of beliefs, the records from that time also come out of that context. Furthermore, history in those days was not noted for its accuracy; that is, in its attention to dates, places, and events. Anyone who believes that the *Book of Joshua* is an exact record of what actually happened at Jericho must also reconcile the apparent cruelty and barbarism of Yahweh (the killing of women and children, even babies) with the loving-kindness of the God of Christian faith. Therefore, the Deuteronomic histories were not passed down to us with the same objectives as our modern histories. The object of the ancient accounts was to show that Yahweh was present to the Israelites as long as the people were faithful to him. When they strayed from this devotion and began to worship alien gods, Yahweh did not abandon Israel, but its people were duly punished for their sins.

Even the New Testament was not written with an eye for historical accuracy. That is not to say that many of the described events did not actually occur. But historical accuracy was not the primary goal of the evangelists. Their first concern was to reveal to the world the good news of Jesus the Christ: his message of love, sacrifice, repentance, and eternal life. Each of the evangelists, therefore, emphasized the basic message of the Jesus tradition in different ways. Each evangelist had different problems within his particular community, and each of them addressed those difficulties in a particular way. Mark, for example, emphasized the importance of a suffering discipleship. As Jesus suffered, so must the followers of Jesus expect to suffer. Luke emphasized prayer in his Gospel, and Matthew had a tendency toward more apocalyptic imagery. What is being discussed here is *redaction criticism,* or in nonscholarly terms, the editing of the Jesus tradition to suit a particular communal need.

The Gospel of John emphasized the divinity of Christ, whereas the Synoptic Gospels (Matthew, Mark, and Luke) emphasized Jesus' humanity. None of the Gospels deny the humanity of Jesus or his divinity, but for reasons of their own, the authors chose to feature certain aspects of the tradition more than others. But the evangelists made mistakes as well; sometimes it was geographical, sometimes it was in the exact date of an event. Compare the time of the crucifixion of Jesus in John's Gospel with that of the Synoptics, for example. Compare also the names of the apostles (disciples in John), how Judas Iscariot died, or even the number of times the cock crows. The point is that none of this really matters as far as the basic intent of the evangelists was concerned. One can get hung up on such details, and in so doing bring only confusion into the picture of what the Jesus tradition is *really* about.

If you recall from chapter 3, Archbishop Ussher used the Book of Genesis as a scientific document, dating God's act of creation at 4004 BC. The Bible, contrary to such perceptions, was written by human beings limited to the constraints of their time and culture. The Hebrew authors, regardless of the inspired nature of their writing, were not scientists and did not write about scientific matters. Other than the fact that God created the entire universe, including our Earth, there is nothing in the Book of Genesis that tells us exactly when or precisely how this was done. One can look for some special interpretation of "let there be light" (Gen 1:3), such as the big bang, or "let the earth bring forth all kinds of living creatures" (Gen 1:24), as supportive of organic evolution. But this would be just as inappropriate as adding up all the ages of the various people of the Book of Genesis in order to arrive at a figure for the age of the Earth. It is simply not wise, in the opinion of most scholars, to use the Bible as evidence *for* or *against* any modern theory.

Thus, we end up with the only possible conclusion: that many individuals, overly zealous in their conservative positions, are limiting God's power of creation to their individually conceived notions about what the Bible means or intends to mean. Where these literalist ideas come from, I am not sure; even as early as the writings of the Apostolic Fathers, the allegory was a common means of interpreting the Old Testament (Shackleford, *The Biblical Heart*, 215). In many instances the conservative stance is not so much a defense of biblical integrity, but a distrust of scientific data. Scientists, unfortunately, are often perceived by many as atheists who are out to discredit the "Bible thumpers" at any cost. Certainly some scientists fit that description, but I can assure you, from my experience of over thirty-five years as a scientist and teacher, they are in the minority. Nevertheless, the perception of science as the enemy is another demon that haunts the marriage bed of science and religion.

DEMONS THAT LIMIT THE POWER OF THE HUMAN INTELLECT

Just as the biblical literalists, unconsciously or otherwise, limit the power of God in their defense of conservatism, so too do they limit the power of the God-given human intellect. It is true, as the apostle Paul says, that the wisdom of God is not the wisdom of humankind (1 Cor 2:6–8), but this does not diminish, or in any way mediate against, human wisdom. Rather, the passages in First Corinthians are stating a simple fact: that God's wisdom is different from human wisdom. God's wisdom is different from ours because it is greater, but also because it is *different in kind*. We may, for example, increase the power of a telescope, or invent a better one, and see the terrain of the planet Mars to better advantage. But no matter how we may increase the power of the intellect, it is still human intellect and, as such, can never approach the wisdom of God because the wisdom of God is a different wisdom. This, I believe, is what Paul is trying to tell us. Still, that leaves humankind with a wealth of brain power with which to explore the created universe. We cannot approach the power of God's wisdom, but the human species does a pretty good job of studying the manifestations of that wisdom.

Not only are scientists doing important work in their study of nature, they are also probing the created sacraments of God. It doesn't matter if these investigations involve chemical bonding, hormonal influences, atomic nuclei, or astrophysical phenomena. It all boils down to the study of God's creation, no matter how one looks at it. Even the atheistic scientist studies God's creation, although he would call it something else.

Is it, therefore, correct and appropriate to be suspicious of the scientist's conclusions? Of course it is, especially if they are new and untested. It was quite natural to be skeptical of Einstein's relativity theory until numerous experiments proved, at least for the most part, that he was correct. One can hardly argue with the $E=MC^2$ formula after seeing an atomic bomb explode. Likewise, every time we turn on a light bulb or a television, we can hardly doubt the flow of electricity into that mechanism, even though we do not see directly the current that animates it.

In my understanding, most Christians believe that God gave us an intellect with some purpose in mind, and that this gift, like the gift of faith, is a part of God's strategy for salvation. I cannot see any other explanation for those who accept a personal God. We must be destined to work out our salvation within the context of faith and intellect cooperating in the search for human authenticity. Otherwise, why not bring on the apocalypse, "wipe away every tear," and simply condemn all the evil people of the world. Would everything then be made all right? I get the impression that this "wipe away every tear" mindset is all too prevalent among some Christian groups. They seem to be waiting around for the Almighty to come on a cloud, with horns tooting, angels singing, and other appropriate sound effects, to set everything straight. Granting that God is full of surprises (Jesus, the God-man was a surprise to those expecting a certain kind of messiah), I believe that literal assumptions taken from the Book of the Apocalypse (or the Book of Daniel) can be misleading.

This mind-set takes away the emphasis from what should be the most important focal point of Christianity, namely, the crucifixion of Jesus. The "First Coming," in my opinion, is what Christians should dwell upon because this puts the ball back in our court. We have the faith—now what are we going to do with it? Are we going to sit around and wait for the Parousia, the Second Coming, to solve all our problems, or are we going to make use of the intellect to better understand what we believe? Science and reason, religion and faith—these are the tools of human salvation, tools that lead us to a clearer understanding of God's strategic role on the stage of creation. Otherwise, what reason is there for our existence? Would God be out to confuse us, giving us tools that don't work, gifts that are meaningless?

I have heard it said, back when the discovery of fossils became known to the general population, that some clergyman explained fossils in this way: "Well, the devil put them there to confuse us." And I suppose one could put that spin on all of existence. Certainly, free will and sin, suffering and death, storms and earthquakes are enough to make us wonder what life is really all about. Why does God send us (allow) these things anyway? Isn't it hard enough for us to save our souls without these natural disasters, without these sinful people?

The answer, of course, is that free will and any resultant sin, as well as natural disasters, are all part of the necessary struggle for survival, all a part of God's strategy for creation's fulfillment. Science and faith play important and interdependent roles in this struggle. Science develops along the lines of helping in the task of taming the environment, dealing with the harshness of weather, giving us comfortable shelter against storms, and providing us with the time to think about the meaning of the adversities in our lives. Faith also helps us in dealing with the internal storms, the emotional and painful experiences of being a human creature. Above all, religious faith assists individuals in integrating the bad and the good of life and putting it all in proper perspective.

Were it not for these storms, internal as well as external, mental as well as physical, we would simply vegetate and accomplish nothing. This observation was one of the seminal contributions of Arnold Toynbee in *A Study of History*. Humankind, as difficult as it may be to understand, needs some degree of adversity to make progress in civilization. Adversity, therefore, is a stimulus to progress, and although it may seem unfortunate, this includes suffering. Now, nobody wants to suffer, and no sane person goes out of his or her way to seek out suffering for its own sake. Most would agree, however, that we grow and mature as a result of suffering, as tragic as it may seem at the time it occurs.

Humanity would never have progressed beyond the most primitive level of existence if all one had to do was reach out and grab food from the nearest tree, while living in a land where the temperature was always comfortable. There would be no need for clothing in this hypothetical land, and there would be no storms or earthquakes. What I have just described, of course, is the Garden of Eden, Paradise. But because we had free will, we were expelled from Paradise, as the Book of Genesis tells us, because humankind wanted to be like God. We wanted to set our own priorities. We desired knowledge of good and evil. Simply put, the Garden of Eden myth tells of the consequences of our human freedom.

But free will is absolutely necessary for goodness as well as evil. Unless we have a choice between the two, we would not be truly human. We would not be created in the image of God. We would be no better that automated bags of biochemicals. We would be robots, simply put, and who can conceive of a robot, a machine with no free will, that is capable of love? That is what free will is all about, *love*; the love of God and the love of neighbor. That is why we experience storms and suffering, internal and external. Without God's strategy, we would never learn to love. All children must grow up to reach adulthood. The children of God must grow up as well, leaving the Garden of Eden to become, truly and authentically, human.

To become authentically human, to reach our full potential as the children of God, we must use the tools of survival and growth that have been given to us, the most important of which are science and religion. Not only must we individually learn to use these tools, it is also imperative that humanity learn to use them together as a cooperative effort. It is like the farmer who prepares the soil properly before sowing the seeds. Science works with the reality of material creation; religion with immaterial creation. Science prepares the soil; religion sows the seeds.

DEMONS THAT LIMIT RELIGIOUS FAITH

Not long ago a man in Dadeville, Alabama, lost a Bible-quoting contest. He was so enraged, police said, that he shot in the face the man who had beaten him in the contest (reported in *The Mobile Register*, July 19, 1996). This is a good example of how focusing one's attention on the narrower aspects of religion can lead to fanaticism. It is the wrong way to approach any religion because constricted views in religion lead to intolerance, fanaticism, and to what I am calling religious idolatry. It does not have to be a fixation on the Bible, as in this example, to constitute religious narrow-mindedness. There are many ways that one can focus in on some minor aspect of faith, and make it into a fixation that colors the entire religious outlook. In saying these things, I do not intend to imply that any of us are totally immune to similar fixations. Most of us have gone down that road, when at times our entire religious life seems to revolve around charitable works, reports of miraculous occurrences, biblical passages, inspiring sermons, or the ministers, priests or rabbis we know. It is this kind of narrowness of vision that stifles growth, even blinds us to the bigger picture of things to come.

One of the most common fixations comes in the form of a religious code, the do's and don'ts of religion. The laws, or religious code, can be thought of as a fence that encircles and guards a certain set of values. Usually these values are articulated in a religious creed. Thus, the religious creed is a basic view of reality that the fence-code is designed to protect. All too often, however, we tend to look upon the rules and regulations in the same way as we do the religious values, or creed. When we do this, it amounts to worshipping the fence instead of what the fence encircles. It is very easy to find oneself drifting in the direction of worshipping the rules and regulations, even letting these do's and don'ts define what religion means to us. It can trap us, if we are not careful, because it leads to a pernicious kind of idolatry from which we find it difficult, if not impossible, to escape. This kind of idolatry is particularly deadly because the entrapped person does not recognize that he or she is entangled in this web of legalistic religion. They believe, most sincerely, that they are doing the right thing, since they are following all the rules and regulations.

Look at it this way. Suppose a man gets out of bed every morning and says his prayers because that is what he is supposed to do. In those prayers he makes a verbal list of all the temptations he is to avoid on that day, and all the do's and don'ts he wants to remember. But in following this routine he is, at the same time, reminding himself of all the delectable temptations that he should be trying to forget. The apostle Paul speaks eloquently of this very problem.

> What then should we say? That the law is sin? By no means! Yet, if it had not been for the law, I would not have known sin. I would not have known what it is to covet if the law had not said, "You shall not covet." But sin, seizing an opportunity in the commandment, produced in me all kinds of covetousness. Apart from the law sin lies dead. I was once alive apart from the law, but when the commandment came, sin revived and I died, and the very commandment that promised life proved to be death to me. For sin, seizing an opportunity in the commandment, deceived me and through it killed me. (Rom 7:7–11)

Paul devotes most of his Letter to the Galatians to this subject. He was very angry with the churches in Galatia because they (apparently) had allowed themselves to be misled by a group of Jewish Christians who came along after Paul's visit. This group (scholars call them *Judaizers*) evidently told the Galatians that Paul was wrong in not insisting on circumcision. We also gather, from Paul's response to the problem, that this group told the Galatians they must observe all the Jewish laws, including circumcision, before they could become bona fide Christians. In effect, they must become Jews before they would be eligible to be Christians.

Paul's angry response boils down to two important issues. First, the Galatians were trying to receive the Spirit by way of the Law, and this is not what Christianity is all about. Paul's Letter to the Galatians has been called the Magna Carta of Christian freedom. Christ came to free us from the Law. There is nothing wrong with the Law, Paul insists, but it is impotent. Even as a list of guidelines, it can do nothing of benefit toward salvation.

Paul told the Galatians they could not receive the Spirit out of the Law. In modern parlance, the Galatians were putting the cart before the horse. If they accepted the loving sacrifice of Christ, they would, out of love for Christ, do the right thing. They did not need all the laws of the Pharisees to tell them the importance of loving God and neighbor.

Second, the Judaizers were making an idol of the Law. They wanted the Galatians to worship the fence, rather than the values the fence was designed to protect. Paul, as a devout Jewish Pharisee before his conversion experience, knew the dangers of this legalistic approach to religion as well as anyone. But he had escaped from this trap, not by his own efforts, but by the grace of God in the form of his conversion experience. He reports this event in his letters, and Luke describes it in the Acts of the Apostles. To Paul the old laws of the Pharisees belonged to a previous age, and had no place in the new age and the new creation that had begun with Christ.

Paul had the opposite problem in Corinth that had occurred in Galatia. In Corinth there were those who carried the idea of Christian freedom to the absurd (1 Cor 6:12–20). In these verses he makes it clear that our bodies are the temples of the Holy Spirit, and when we dishonor our bodies we are dishonoring Christ. Therefore, everything may be lawful but not everything is beneficial (6:12). As Paul solved one problem, another rose up in its place.

The apostle Paul was not some isolated scholar who sat up nights by oil-lamp writing theological treatises. He is the premiere theologian of the New Testament, and his great insights came from experience. We can look around us, examine the circumstances of our time just as Paul did, and garner some of the same types of insights. We can gain a lot of wisdom simply by reading the newspaper, especially if one looks at current events from a faith perspective.

Terrorism is among the most devastating effects of religious narrow-mindedness. I am sitting here writing with the memory of bombs and destroyed aircraft fresh on my mind. One morning I awoke to a newspaper headline that read "Olympic Park hit by blast." It is no secret that many, if not most, acts of terrorism are inspired by religious bigotry. It is certainly true that economic conditions may be at the root of the problem, but in the end it is religion that gets the lion's share of the blame. Perhaps the most difficult aspect of terrorist acts to understand is the religious intolerance and hatred at the bottom of it all. Religion is supposed to be about loving one another, even loving one's enemy.

It seems no religion is immune to such violence and desecration. In the Western world, Roman Catholics, Protestants, Jews, and Muslims are equally involved in such dishonorable activities. One could argue, of course, that the perpetrators are religious only in name, that no truly religious person, no authentically human person, could possibly justify these acts. We should label them, in fact, the work of so-called Christians, or so-called Jews, or so-called Muslims. Regardless of that argument, there are many in this world who are totally turned off by religion because of what they see as religious hypocrisy. I see it not so much as hypocrisy as narrow-mindedness. We are simply not teaching tolerance of other religious views as we should be.

You and I belong to a particular religion because we believe it relates to a view of reality that comes closest to the truth (I use religion here in the broadest sense to include such diverse value systems as secular humanism). But if and when a religion teaches that it is the sole possessor of all truth, revealed or otherwise, and that no other religion has any truth to it, then the ministers of that religion have abandoned reason. Reason and faith should go hand in hand. They should complement one another, not compete in a contest where one wins and the other loses. Abandoning reason in the name of faith is to forsake growth and maturity. It is like a five-year-old declaring that he or she wants to remain the same age, never to become an adult. Theology is, after all, *faith seeking understanding*, and is grounded in the most basic questions and needs of the human person. Theology means, in the basic sense of the word, a rational discourse about God, which is what is being attempted on these pages.

The crucial element in the study of God—that is, theology—is personal faith. One who does not have the gift of faith will be intractable to any suggestions theology might make, especially about the existence of a loving, compassionate God. Avery Dulles (*The Craft of Theology*, 7) sees today's, or "postcritical," theology as beginning with the presupposition of faith, and as a fundamental attitude of trust, not of suspicion. It is the attitude of suspicion (an offspring of narrow-mindedness) that fosters the terrorist mentality. It is poisonous to any religious truth because it distorts its value system to the breaking point.

Swiss theologian Hans Küng argues that every human being, faced with an uncertain reality, must opt for a positive or negative attitude toward life (*Foundation of Theological Study*, 80). There must be, therefore, a fundamental trust or distrust in existence. Fundamental trust is the only rational and psychologically healthy stance, but we are not forced into an attitude of trust: we must freely choose it. Belief in God means that fundamental trust has an ultimate rational ground.

The underlying and sustaining dynamic of all religions is the act of *faith*, the staking of life and the casting of meaning on that which is partially seen, partially unseen. Since faith involves an interpretive approach to reality, it is the very lifeblood of the religious experience. Faith in the broad sense encompasses more than the purely religious dimension. It is integral to all human activity. Narrow-mindedness, therefore, is the enemy of any faith, religious faith in particular. It is, indeed, the demon that limits human growth because it stifles belief in anything but misunderstanding and mistrust. Finally, narrow-mindedness is the demon that engenders violence against those who do not possess the selfsame distorted view of reality.

Narrow-mindedness, to be sure, is not limited to religion. It applies to any outlook on reality, including value systems based on science or secular humanism. The next chapter will look at the demons of science, particularly those that deny aspects of reality on which codes of behavior are based.

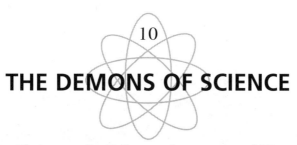

THE DEMONS OF SCIENCE

Since Christ was the God-man, the meaning of His crucifixion cannot be that the Jews happened, by chance, to be
perverse at that time, and Christ, so to speak, an unfortunate victim of circumstance. No, what happened to Christ
is of universal character, it demonstrates the obduracy of
the whole human race; the same thing will always happen
to Him.   —Søren Kierkegaard

In a certain sense, humanity does continue to crucify God on a
daily basis. In this I agree with Ronald Rolheiser that there exists in
modern society an unbridled narcissism and pragmatism that kills
God over and over, precluding the sense of God's presence in our
everyday life *(The Shattered Lantern)*. It seems an enormous effort is
made in modern society just to avoid thinking about God because
human consciousness has been hardened to the religious sensitivity
we once had. Science, along with religious narrow-mindedness, must
bear a heavy responsibility for this loss and for the death of God
among so many in our society. These are the demons that murder
God, that disfigure the dream of final unity in all things. In this chapter I intend to expose the demons of science just as I have already
attempted to expose them within our religious perceptions.

Science consists in efforts that measure, balance, weigh, and
examine all manner of experimental data, reaching conclusions that
tell us something of the natural world in which we live. It is neither
moral nor amoral, nor does it convey to its practitioners any sense of
what is right or wrong, except as it might relate to the consistency or
reproducibility of its data. Moral responsibility and ethical sensibility
must come from outside the discipline. Nevertheless, scientists are
obliged to demonstrate this moral and ethical sense, or the science

they practice would be a worthless pursuit. How could one trust the data? How could one believe in anything science tells us if the ethics of the scientific community was always in doubt?

DEMONS THAT LIMIT THE DIMENSIONS OF REALITY

The demons of science would not be quite so detrimental if they were limited only to the perceptions of scientists. Unfortunately, it is sometimes the nonscientist who is most enamored with science and, in many cases, believes its claims with few reservations. But to what extent is it fitting and proper to base our actions on science's lofty accomplishments? Science allows us to flip the switch, to turn on modernity: lights on, lights off. Ironically, it gives us a fast car in which to kill ourselves, while it keeps us more healthy than at any other time in history. This contradictory example, and other misconceptions, hardly break the surface of what science means to the average citizen.

When I speak of the demons of science, I am by no means referring just to scientific advancements. I am most often referring to the pervasive *influence* of science on the general public, most of whom do not know how to distinguish between a molecule and a tissue, the thymus and the spleen, a star and a galaxy, the big bang and the big crunch. It is this segment of the population who most often makes an idol of science, particularly its wondrous and myriad inventions. Science has encouraged us to live day to day as an agglomeration of functions. So much time for work, so much for play, sex, and relaxation, but almost no time to think and pray about ultimate questions, or to even recognize the need for prayer. It is this disregard, brought on by so much business, so much attention to physiological needs to the neglect of eternal concerns, that constitutes the demonic pathology in the scientific milieu of our society.

It is perhaps the fault of scientists that they do not emphasize enough the limits of science. They are so consumed with the business of getting research dollars, so eager to report all the good things they have done, that the general public does not understand that science has merely picked up a grain of sand off the cosmic beach. There is yet an entire beach of unknowns that confront the darlings of science, and beyond that an entire ocean of unknowns that science will never even know are there, much less understand. We have questions in science now that prompt answers in theological terms, and that is why there is so much God-talk in books written by scientists. The problem here is that scientists (qua scientists) are not qualified to answer theological questions, although they attempt to do so on a regular basis. Be that as it may, I find John Horgan's *The End of Science* encouraging because it opens the door to the discussion of dimensions beyond the physical, material universe. The unfortunate aspect of most works in this genre, however, is that the science is too sophisticated for the average person to grasp. This mentality among scientists living in the world of "on" and "off" switches does not recognize that the god of science is profoundly limited.

In my book *The Biblical Heart*, I discussed an interview on Public Television that profiled the life of Richard Feynman as "the best mind since Einstein." I have the greatest respect for devoted scientists such as Feynman who, nevertheless, appear to derive their ethics and, consequently, their behavior, out of a godless universe. He said as much in his interview on PBS, not long before he died of cancer. That is not to say that he was an evil person or had a "bad" set of ethics. To the contrary, he seemed to have been a decent person who was very much concerned for others. On the show he confessed a sense of guilt for his part in building the atomic bomb, which he at first justified as a means of ending the atrocities of Nazi Germany. After Germany was defeated, however, he continued to work on the project without reexamining the morality of doing so, and for this activity he felt a great deal of culpability.

Richard Feynman was a man who lived and breathed physics. He examined all problematic avenues in terms of possible solutions within this framework. The existence of a personal God was not something solvable by physics and, accordingly, Feynman simply moved on to problems that he could solve. Now, this is all well and good because there are many problems, including those of a personal God, an afterlife, and so on, that are unsolvable in terms of the scientific method. What saddened me somewhat as I watched the program was that Feynman, since he could not solve the questions of God and eternal life, concluded that creation existed outside any kind of redemptive power.

What seems to be an even more basic problem, insofar as the world of science is concerned, is a case of paradigm worship. One can be so locked into a particular habit of thinking (a kind of Hegelian Zeitgeist) that it becomes impossible to see beyond that horizon. Such thinking becomes for the individual a paradigm idolatry, a worship of the physical sciences as somehow encompassing all of reality.

Given that religion is not the proper object of physicochemical experimentation, science cannot venture beyond the limits of its methods, regardless of how rigorous or sophisticated the discipline might be. Certainly it is proper, even necessary, that science endeavor to stretch its boundaries and expand its horizons. But when it reaches its limits, beyond which there is no possibility of further progress, this is a discovery in itself. It is here that the limitless beckons to human-kind across the chasm between types of wisdom (more on this later). What may seem troubling to the religious communities is the arro-gance of some scientists who would never admit to any such limits. That is why John Horgan's book *The End of Science* is refreshing—it admits to these barriers, and even takes the trouble to define some of them.

In all scientific experiments, it is necessary to somehow get out-side the specimen being studied. In order to examine an animal cell, for example, the researcher has to remove the cell from the animal, place it under a microscope, perhaps stain it with a suitable dye, then describe the structures he or she sees. The biochemist would have to grind up the cell and look for the presence of proteins, fats, amino acids, sugars, hormones, and so on. Thus, it is necessary to destroy the living unit to learn all that is possible to know about that particular cell. But in destroying the cell, the investigator has changed its nature and thereby has lost the ability to totally understand the living speci-men. Scientific analysis, therefore, has that built-in limitation and always will to some extent.

The closer we approach the very basis of life, or the very basis of material existence, the more this principle holds true. We must some-how get outside the object of the experiment in order to understand it from the limited point of view of science. Carrying this a little fur-ther, to reach a thorough appreciation of matter and energy, the sci-entist would somehow have to become nonmaterial to do so. In other words, to really understand the fundamental forces and basic nature of matter, a *spiritual* being would be required to do the experiment. This is indeed a limitation of the scientific method, one which we don't hear enough of from the lips of scientists.

Is evolution a process of blind chance, or is there an intelligence behind it? What happened before the big bang? Why is there something rather than nothing? Is there truly a spiritual dimension to existence of which the prophets and mystics speak? Why do not more investigators recognize that it is a worthy objective to define the limits of empirical science? Why not write a speculative work about the mysteries of the universe that will never be solved by scientific methods? Let scientists try to shoot down these theories, argue fundamental points, and reach tentative conclusions about the *interface* between physics and metaphysics, between what is knowable and unknowable.

We have come a long way since the eighteenth century, when there was such confidence in science that there seemed to be no mysteries, only things yet to be discovered. The hangover from that time is the absolute disdain of many scientists for anything religious. It is this kind of macho scientist who does not need God or any of the trappings of religion. He or she is perfectly happy living in a godless world where science rules. When science rules, of course, the scientist becomes the ruler, if not the philosopher king.

I do not intend to paint scientists as so tied to their discipline that they refuse to consider theological questions. Many believe in a loving, personal God, and some who do not, wish they could. But scientists, like the average modern person, are full of the business of day-to-day activities. They may be so bound up in a personal timetable and in their physical life that theological questions are simply pushed to the side. In this sense, the scientist is no different from the average nonscientist.

DEMONS THAT THREATEN HUMAN EXISTENCE

Some of the shine and novelty wore off the darlings of science in the centuries after the Enlightenment. Then came the industrial revolution, with its child labor, slums, and pollution. War became more sophisticated as bombs and artillery were designed to kill more people. But the really devastating weapon of mass destruction, the nuclear bomb, raised questions that had never crossed the minds of the vast majority of humankind. Now it was possible to wipe out the human species. As one particular leader was quoted as saying, if a nuclear war ever occurs, the lucky ones will be the ones killed instantly. The rest will die slowly, either from radiation sickness or from the long aftermath of a nuclear winter.

In a way, as horrible as a nuclear war would be, one can detect a saving strategy in it for humankind. For the first time humanity had been given a tool of destruction that could wipe out the human species. Never before in human history had there been such a potential for mass extinction as in the nuclear arsenals of the major powers of the world. Intercontinental missiles, loaded with multiple nuclear warheads bristled the landscape of the United States and the Soviet Union (now Russia), while the smaller powers rushed headlong into building their own complement of nuclear weapons. Every country has deemed it necessary to join the nuclear-power club.

The situation was, and still is, a crisis of truly cataclysmic proportions. Use the bomb on another country and run the risk of an unprecedented retaliation. Use the bomb on a close neighbor and just the radiation from it could kill millions of one's own people. It is, therefore, a time in which the human race is forced to grow and mature a little, or risk worldwide genocide. War, at least on a global scale, has become so horrible to contemplate that if World War III should occur, it would undoubtedly be the last war: there would be no people left on Earth to start World War IV.

I see in this situation a message from God: "Okay, so I have given you, the human creature, the intellect to study and learn about the material world in which you live. Now you have discovered a force of nature that can destroy all that I have given you. Are you yet so barbaric and unfeeling that you would dare demolish everything I have created? Show me that you have grown up a little from the time when war was a glorious enterprise, when killing your brothers and sisters was a thrill to boast about."

God indeed is present and speaks to us in history. God has set into motion a dialectic between science and religion, between the seen and the unseen, between the sacred and the profane. But we must have the sense and the humility to recognize this strategy, this dialectic, which God has set in motion, the ultimate purpose of which is to help us to find the way "back home." The atheist does not have to accept that it is God that sets the stage, creating this dramatic crucible of history. Nevertheless, it is a test of human survival. Has our will to survive as a species outgrown our lust for killing? That is the question and the test, regardless of one's faith in God. It is a critical point in the history of humankind, a pivotal crisis, a dialectical crucible in which religion and science must learn to work together.

The crisis of nuclear war is a difficult hurdle for us, but there will be other, even greater tests that may challenge the limits of our endurance. I am not speaking in this instance of something I foresee as an even greater weapon of war. No, it is more subtle than a bomb, slower to kill its target, and yet more devastating in the end. The problem takes the form of two critical perspectives, one internal, one external. Both forms are like slow, yet lethal cancers eating away at the environment, one infecting the balance of nature and the other infecting genetics.

The Balance of Nature, the External Environment

We are continually hearing news about the environment: the torching of Amazon forests, crude-oil spills, industrial pollution, acid rain, the diminished ozone layer, and so on. One day we will have to come to grips with our greed for riches, bigger and better cars and boats, more shopping centers, and disposable materials that produce mountains of garbage. This wastefulness and greed are demons that threaten our existence, more slowly, but just as certainly, as nuclear weapons. What has science to do with this? Almost everything. Without science most of the damage to the environment would not have been possible, or even entered our heads. Without science we would still be living in a preindustrial civilization. There would be no paper mills or saw mills, no plastic containers or disposable diapers, no gigantic shopping centers and skyscrapers, all of which place enormous demands on the environment. Am I saying all these modern things are intrinsically bad? Of course not. Modernity, with all its scientific and technological trappings, is part of our historical momentum.

It seems pretty obvious, however, that sometime and somehow we must apply the brakes. Runaway growth must come to a stop, or at least level off, and reach a stable balance between our desire for progress and the health of the environment. This is another worldwide crisis of cataclysmic proportions, with all the more potential for destructiveness because of its subtle and gradual movement, mostly unnoticed by the masses. Scientists deserve a lot of credit on this issue. Although the fruits of science and invention have given birth to unbridled industrial growth and nuclear weaponry, individual scientists have been at the forefront in warning the public of its potential dangers. Ironically then, it is the scientist who opens Pandora's box, then rushes to close the lid by warning the public before too much damage is done. In large part, civilization moves forward, or backward, depending on how wide the lid is opened and how well we react to the new discoveries. Pandora, as the myth reveals, was a person of exceeding curiosity, and this describes precisely the typical scientists of the world. We were all, to a greater or lesser extent, created with natural curiosity. It just so happens that most scientists are overly endowed with this quality.

The Balance of Nature, the Internal Environment

Here we look at another, even more subtle demon of science: How do we control the temptation to tamper with the human genome beyond what is in our best interest as a species? How do we not compromise the dignity and sanctity of human life? We are reaching the point in genetics research at which these questions pose crucial moral dilemmas. Working to heal genetically based diseases, such as diabetes mellitus or cystic fibrosis, is, of course, admirable. But in learning how to manipulate certain nucleotides of DNA to deactivate bad genes, perhaps even to replace them with good genes, we also learn to do the same thing with *normal* genes. Here is the great temptation to play God and to experiment with the human genome in an inappropriate way, justifying the research on the basis of "improving the human race" or "ridding society of the burden of imperfect babies."

This will never happen, some might say. We will never tamper with the normal genetic makeup of a person. Somehow I find no comfort in that assumption. First of all, who decides what is "normal." Do we consider individuals with low intelligence abnormal? Should we dream of creating a race of geniuses? What about freckles, eye color, or the size of the nose? Where do we draw the line? Should parents be the ones to make these major decisions about the intelligence level

112

of a child, personality traits, longevity, and so on? The problem does not stop with genetically altered offspring. Suppose the result of such manipulations also affects the gametes, such as an egg or sperm cell, so that the altered genes are passed on to the next generation? Then the results of the genetic changes will be passed on to successive generations, long after the original parents are dead, perhaps forgotten. Such a scenario is food for serious thought. It already represents a bountiful harvest for science-fiction novelists.

Once we have done something like this, how do we undo it? How do we put the genie back in the bottle? Let us suppose that long-term effects of a certain genetic change include devastating personality defects, certainly a potential threat to the human species as we know it. At some future date, perhaps it will be genetically altered individuals, perhaps the ones with the personality defects, making the decisions. The mistakes of the past could be magnified. The problem is immense because we cannot simply kill off our mistakes when they involve human beings. The difficulties are ineluctable because science cannot predict with any acceptable degree of precision the long-term effects of new drugs, much less genetic manipulations, that may be passed on to future generations.

Suppose we postulate a purely mechanistic world in which humankind controls the future course of human evolution. It might seem a reasonable ambition if there were no moral or ethical issues to consider. But we do not live in a purely mechanistic, godless world, according to the beliefs of a vast majority of the world's population. So we must learn that science has its limits, not always in terms of what is possible, but sometimes in terms of what is ethically and morally responsible, because the entire course of history is at stake.

A HISTORICAL PERSPECTIVE

Arnold Toynbee (*A Study of History*) is known for his comparison of historical progress to a point on the rim of a wheel. As the wheel moves forward, the point at the edge of the wheel moves up and down, and at times seems to move backwards. All along, however, the wheel moves forward, and civilization (the point on the wheel) moves along with it, sometimes more slowly, at times more rapidly. It might be said that the wheel itself is science, while the steering mechanism is religion, our moral and ethical concerns. However, the engine that drives the wagon (and thus the wheel) is humankind, with all its propensity for frailty, personal failure, and imperfection. Humanity, in this metaphorical sense, has been given dominion over its historical destiny, to accelerate the engine and to steer the wheel of history in the right direction. It is a jolting, narrow road on which the wagon must move, through treacherous, unknown country.

Religious consciousness—a sensibility to what is good and ultimately true; a faith in the righteousness of that final goal waiting for us at the end of the road—is the ideal steering mechanism. Without science and religion working together, however, little progress, if any, is possible. The wheels of science are continually analyzing and evaluating the driving conditions—and, in fact, the road itself. Without science, humankind would never know the road or its dangerous pitfalls, and yet it is a journey we must make. It is the strategy of God to bring us home to live in his kingdom. There are no shortcuts, and we cannot get to our destination without the curiosity of science or the faith of religion. The two must work together to make our journey here on Earth a success.

I have spoken of the dialectic between science and religion, which I believe to be a necessary ingredient of God's saving strategy for humankind. Unfortunately, when arguments break out between these two forces, the mentality seems to prevail that someone must win the argument and the other party must lose. It is a win/lose situation where no one profits from the dialogue, and all parties get angry. Letters to newspaper editors are all too frequently in this vein. This mentality is, "Take no prisoners, damn it!" But what if there is some truth to both sides? Specious arguments delivered in anger do nothing to enhance the learning possibilities of the disagreement. What has happened to our abilities in this regard? Is our faith so weak, or our position so arrogant, that we cannot even seek to understand another's viewpoint? It seems we have a lot of growing up to do when it comes to science versus religion. Narrow-minded people of faith are much like the arrogant scientist in this respect.

When we come to the collective realization that the dialectic is a learning process, as well as a saving process, then we will have made real progress. The demons will have been identified and expelled from the marriage bed. And the marriage of science and religion will have been consummated. I wish I were among those who see, more clearly than I ever could, this idea of a perfecting dialectic. Those who comprehend it with such clarity are the great poets and mystics of the world, the sages and prophetic voices who, like John the Baptist, cry out in a wilderness of human indifference. These are the few who truly understand the orientation of time and its privileged axis. These are the ones who have glimpsed the strategy of God, not just in an intellectual sense, but with their hearts as well.

In the end, science is a system of observations built on the shoulders of those who preceded our generation. Science in its most honorable of enterprises—a poultice for the wounded, food for the poor, compassion for the sick—does not arrive at its charity out of weights and measures, or its empirical data. It does so because it sees a glimmer, the faintest acknowledgment of all that is good and trustworthy in creation and in the basic sanity of religious beliefs. Scientists, after all, do not live and operate in a vacuum. The influence of the highest ethical calling hangs over their shoulders: "Do unto others as you would have them do unto you." This credo of all great religions, the doctrine of something higher than all weights and measures and all empirical data, dogs even the most hard-hearted scientist. It is Jesus saying, "Love your neighbor as yourself."

This is not religion, it might be said; it's simply common sense, what everybody should do just to get along, to live side by side without killing one another. If it is religion that makes us do good things, one might ask, Why do religions themselves not observe this common-sense credo? Why are there even religious wars? I don't see scientists blowing up one another, terrorizing innocent civilians, all in the name of science. Yet religions, one could say, have done these terrible things throughout history, and are doing it now.

Yes, we have to admit that human beings do horrible things in the name of religious beliefs. The fact that they do so with the instruments and weapons of science does not alter this terrible reality. In acknowledging it, however, does this say something about the higher goals of religion or, more precisely, the human condition itself? When we examine these facts for what they are, the truth of the matter is that we can blame a lot of things on religion, but also on science. Human beings love a scapegoat, but this does not take the onus from our collective backs. Humankind is imperfect. There is no denying that, and yet we tend to blame the other guy for his lack of perfection. We do not blame Ptolemy for his erroneous ideas about the position of Earth in the universe. Yet we do blame religious leaders for not comprehending the essence of their beliefs perfectly or practicing them flawlessly. Thus, it appears that science and religion are both still growing up. We are brothers and sisters of one reality, whether we like it or not, and as typical brothers and sisters, we fight, almost constantly. That is how it should be up to a point because that is basic to the dialectic we have been discussing all along. When we finally see the dialectic for what it is, I believe humanity will take a giant step forward.

11

SCIENCE, RELIGION, AND DOUBT

> "You have seen lamps, so you imagine a bigger and better lamp and called it the *sun*. You've seen cats, and now you want a bigger and better cat, and it's to be called a *lion*.... And look how you can put nothing into your make-believe without copying it from the real world, this world of mine, which is the only world" [The Witch's response to "proofs" for the existence of *Overworld*].
>
> —C. S. Lewis, *The Silver Chair*

What is the origin of doubt? A number of emotions and events may be attributed to this problem. It is never a simple occurrence. One thing for sure is that we all experience periods of doubt (or radical questioning), and if severe enough, it can be debilitating. It happens to scientists, faithful religious, or any individual who suddenly discovers doubt crashing down upon his or her spiritual integrity. The topic of concern here, however, is science and religion, so I will focus in on doubts that may arise from this perspective. *Spiritual* integrity, as the adjective implies, must involve the integration of all avenues of experience. It is common sense not to divide our perspective on reality into compartments, one for science and one for religion, as though to deny one or the other. Compartmentalizing science and religion into separate mental categories, such that the two are unable to relate, can be dangerous. Whether we like it or not, there is one cosmic and eternal truth that includes all of humanity's endeavors. Science is one of the avenues that support spiritual endeavors, which is, of course, the principal thrust of this book. By the same token, religion, at least its moral and ethical aspects, is necessary for good science. Compartmentalizing them is one origin of doubt.

Doubt is something we all experience, no matter how fleeting or how profound. In many individuals the idea of doubting their faith is so devastating that repression becomes the only safe harbor. To doubt something so fundamental to our identity as a human being—our faith—can be the most frightening of emotions. Because of this fear we may deny that such thoughts ever enter our mind. The fear is that such thoughts, calling into question our dearest traditions, may grow into unmanageable proportions. Indeed, they may precipitate an outright rejection of the faith we hold so close to heart. Fear, then, is followed by feelings of guilt.

A consciousness of fear is the first indication of doubt. The fear is that we will lose our faith, and with that loss, the comfort that our religion has provided, perhaps for most of our adult life. The loss of one's faith can be worse than losing a loved one because it tends to violate our treasured relationships with friends and family. Under these circumstances one might conclude that it would be simpler to pretend that we *never* doubted our faith. That way we could go on with our lives as though nothing had changed.

In my opinion, denial is the worst thing we can do in regard to any reality. For one thing it is not healthy, mentally or physically. Psychologists tell us we must confront our fears and other troublesome thoughts because that is the only way we can deal with them effectively. We may need to get help in overcoming these emotions, but that is not a bad or shameful way to go. We will always have some lingering doubts, and if we deny them, we may be faced with a continuing cycle of doubt, fear, and repression.

I have found a combination of healthy ways to confront these troublesome thoughts, but I hasten to add that I am not a professional in this area of psychology. What I am about to say stems from a long life of experience, rather than professional insight.

First of all, it helps to think of doubt as a shadow, one that shows the reality of what is doubted, in this case, one's faith. We cannot doubt something that has no reality or no existence. In this case the doubt points to the reality of our faith, albeit diminished in our mind's eye. This shadow is not unlike Plato's shadows cast against a cave wall by a campfire outside the cave (*The Republic*). Plato likened the material universe we see around us to mere shadows of the reality that cast the shadows. The real world, according to Plato, consists of that which moves around outside the cave. Thinking of doubts as shadows is a first step in confronting what could become a serious problem.

Another concept with which to battle doubt is hope. One could escape doubt if such a thing as absolute certainty were possible. If one could be absolutely certain of the basic tenets of one's faith, including the promise of personal salvation, it would be easy to set aside any doubts in this regard. But what would become of the concept of Christian hope? One doesn't hope in something if it is a foregone conclusion. A person does not hope he will get a raise in salary if he sees the check go into the mail. He knows he will get it when the mail arrives at his house. Hope is an essential dimension of faith, as the apostle Paul tells us over and over: "For in hope we were saved. Now hope that is seen is not hope. For who hopes for what is seen? But if we hope for what we do not see, we wait for it with patience" (Rom 8:24–25). The claim to absolute certainty in any abstract notion, including the existence of a loving, personal God, strikes me as a display of human arrogance. We cannot *know* with absolute certainty that a personal, loving God exists. Surprisingly, many feel they are not good Christians if they are not absolutely certain of their personal salvation; in fact, this uncertainty is the most normal of human limitations. So why worry about some small fleeting doubts that linger at the boundaries of our consciousness? Why should *we* be above everybody else in not having these moments? To repress our doubting spirit is to deny our very humanity. God did not create us to know everything with certainty, especially belief in his very existence. So where do we turn in moments of grief, fear, and depression when hope seems to be drowned out by nagging doubts, when we experience our "dark nights of the soul"?

Yet another way to combat doubt: One must see the rightness of faith, which, in a way, is the act of *living* one's hope. Then, if possible, one must make sense of faith through the intellect. Simply because we have faith does not mean that we abandon reason. For Christians, a loving, personal God is a comforting view of reality that somehow rings true. The words of Jesus as passed down to us in the gospel accounts resonate with this truth. Even the existence of Jesus the Christ himself makes sense, although the idea of a God-man was "folly" to the pagans who confronted the early Christians. From the point of view of our faith, it makes sense that a loving God would send his Son to become flesh and show us the way, to be our role model. To believe otherwise is to exist in a chaotic world with little meaning. These thoughts that make sense are the ones to cling to in our darkest moments.

We should never forget how to dream. Dreaming is a metaphor for, or an extension of, hoping, in the sense I intend here. Such imaginary thoughts are important and never trivial, especially if one dreams of a better world, one in which love of neighbor is the rule rather than the exception. In this world, human free will is directed toward helping one another instead of hating one another. In this world the greatest joy comes from serving God, enjoying our healthy children, watching them grow up, and enjoying nature's bounty. At all cost we must hold on to such a dream. If there is to be a battle between the power of doubt and the power of dreaming, then the one who dreams will win out every time. Dreaming joined to reason is more powerful than either one alone. It follows also that the unity of reasoning and dreams with faith and hope is an invincible combination. One can dream of almost any reality and believe it so strongly that no amount of argument can convince the dreamer otherwise. That is why dreams (hopes) are so important. They sustain us when we are emotionally drained. Even when we have failed to realize our hopes, or seem to have lost our faith, we almost never lose the capacity to dream.

The existence of a reality that includes a loving, personal God is a vision that defies intellectual proofs, yet a person who lives his or her life according to such a vision will have many followers. Jesus of Nazareth did not use logic and abstract reasoning to teach about his vision of reality. Instead, he lived what he taught. The disciples did not really understand who Jesus was until after his death on the cross, yet they followed him because of the way he lived. He taught with great authority, but this would have meant nothing without his example.

Dreams can be transformed into faith if one believes in the dream strongly enough. Faith, in its broadest sense, is the foundation of all perceived reality: for Christian, Jew, Muslim, Hindu and Buddhist; for saints and sinners; for believers and nonbelievers. We all live in the same reality, and in some measure, at least, we attempt to impose the reality *we* envisage on the general population. Each of us color it differently, but most of us believe it is the same reality, nevertheless. One might ask, of course, can we *create* our own reality? Can we make our own hell on earth? Is it possible that some wishes actually come true? Can we make our own place in God's heaven if we pray for it hard enough and want it badly enough? These things too may be possible, but only if we can dream and have faith in what we dream.

It does no good to blame all the bad things on God, science, ourselves, or some other person. We can only try to become what we are ultimately destined to be, what our faith, informed or uninformed, tells us about reality. It is our calling to *be something*, even if that something merely occupies space, eats, breathes, and eliminates waste. If we choose to be less than what our humanity calls us to be, perhaps it is because of our failure to dream of honorable things, perfect justice, loving-kindness, and the ultimate goodness of all creation. What if we refuse to listen to our dreams and the promptings of faith? What would happen if our sons and daughters never prophesied, or our young men became blinded to new visions, and our old men never dreamed? (See Acts 2:17.)

C. S. Lewis reminds us that there comes a time when one must say to God, "You must do this, I can't" (*Mere Christianity*, 128). The problem with our self-centeredness is the overweening pride (in Greek, *hubris*) we have in our abilities. In such cases, one will ask assistance from scarcely anyone, much less God. That is why we sometimes choose to be slaves to our passions rather than admit to our limitations and personal weaknesses. That is why dreaming of a better life for ourselves, for everyone on this earth and beyond it, is so necessary. As Lewis says:

> Suppose we *have* only dreamed, or made up those things— trees and grass and sun and moon and stars and Aslan himself. Suppose we have. Then all I can say is that, in that case, the made-up things seem a good deal more important than the real ones. Suppose this black pit of a kingdom of yours is the only world. Well, it strikes me as a pretty poor one....We're just babies making up a game if you are right. But four babies playing a game can make a play-world which licks your real world hollow." (Puddleglum, speaking to the Witch; *The Silver Chair*, 191)

121

Faith Seeking Understanding

My last way of confronting doubt, to which even practical atheism should find no obstacle, is the ability to dream of goodness, justice, and a basic respect for human dignity. That is all one can ask for the present, not some concrete system or commitment, or even some vague religious precept. Simply dream that somewhere, somehow, sometime, there exists the quality of goodness, justice, and mutual respect. Then civilized peoples everywhere can proceed from that point to what must be an achievable goal, but to do so, we must learn to dream like children once again (see Matt 18:23).

Today we are told by some philosophers that they see no reason to believe in a God of any kind. In the existence they describe, there is no hope of perfect justice, eternal peace, love, and so on, and especially no hope to ever satisfy the human appetite for these things. All that would be left to us is the gnawing question of why "nature" had planted such an appetite in the human psyche with no means of ever satisfying it. Our only conclusion concerning any reality that excluded a loving, personal God would be that nature is cruel because all the other appetites (excepting this one) are capable of satisfaction. Thus the appetite for food, warmth, sex, family, friends, security, and so on, are goals for which there is a reasonable possibility of acquisition. But nature, because that is all there would be in a world without God, gave us this other meaningless appetite for eternal life. Why, then, has history shown us that we are not alone in this persistent and intense desire for eternity?

The only answer the atheist can give us to this question is, "Well, that's just the way it is." Fortunately, in my experience at least, there are far more scientists who believe in a personal God than those who do not. These friends and colleagues of mine recognize that there are some things for which science will never have an answer. The existence or nonexistence of a personal, loving God, especially a God-man, is one of those unanswerable questions. Indeed, the early Christian church argued over the God-man issue for centuries and continued to do so long after the Nicene Council in AD 325.

When we experience moments of doubt (or radical questioning, if you prefer), our dreams can become our reality, if only to bridge over the times when we feel abandoned by God. In these moments of personal crisis, if we can sustain ourselves with the dream of ultimate goodness, and the cosmic promise that we will eventually share in this vision, then we can survive any challenge the world may present. Indeed, it even seems that we somehow increase in worthiness by clinging to the dream in times of crisis because in doing so we endure (Matt 10:22, 24:13; see also Mark 13:13). By contrast, if we let our doubts get the best of us, we are implicitly accepting the vision of a cruel and unjust world of unmitigated darkness and meaningless chance.

Most of all, in the context of this work, science should never pose a threat to one's equanimity. Science is a gift to humankind from God, not to be feared or reviled. Science is what it is, a *reasonable* way to approach the Creator of all that is and all that will be. As a gift from God, science cannot be a bad thing in itself. The only thing we need fear is the misuse of science by God's human creation. At times, humanity is its own worst enemy. Any of God's gifts can be abused or misused, including human freedom. The abuse of this great gift, human freedom, can only be counterbalanced by the greatest of all gifts, and that is God's self-communication with us. In God's sharing the gift of faith with his human creatures, Christians believe he shares his divinity. In the case of this divine gift, one cannot separate the Gift from the Giver, and that is how we come to be "temples of the Holy Spirit" (2 Cor 3:16).

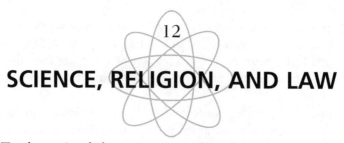

SCIENCE, RELIGION, AND LAW

Teach us, Lord, how to contemplate the sphinx without
succumbing to its spell; how to grasp the mystery hidden
in the womb of death not by a refinement of human doctrine, but in the simple concrete act by which You immerse
Yourself in matter in order to redeem it. By virtue of your
suffering Incarnation disclose to us, and then teach us to
harness jealously for You, the spiritual power of matter.
—Teilhard de Chardin, *Divine Milieu*

Like science, law has been integrally tied to religion from the
beginning of civilization. From the ancient Mesopotamian powers
residing by the Tigris and Euphrates, to the Egyptians along the Nile,
to the Hindus of the Indus river—civilizations have depended upon,
survived, and exploited laws like the rivers by which they flourished.
Thus, not only science and religion, unsophisticated as they may have
been in those early places and times, but also law, were bound
together so tightly and intimately that one could hardly say where one
ended and the other began. In our day as well, this relationship
applies to the laws of nature just as surely as it does to the man-made
ones.

Religion, science, and law expressed most of what life was all
about to the people. Religion told them of the gods, the awesome
supernatural powers that explained creation and their origins as a
people. Primitive science, an extension of their religious beliefs,
solved practical matters, such as when to plant their crops, what the
heavens told them about the seasons of the year, the cyclic nature of
their existence in a strange and often fearsome world. Man-made law
protected them, mostly from one another, so they could plant their
crops, raise their families, and worship their gods. It also served the

purposes of the priests and rulers, and was mostly tailored to their needs and aspirations as leaders of the people. Still, every ruler, even in earliest history, recognized that chaos would reign supreme without laws that governed the people. The law in ancient times was both used and abused, as it is today. It can be a soothing soporific or a cruel scimitar. It can provide protection and security or evoke fear and anxiety. Man-made law was, and still is, multifaceted, variegated, and malleable, a great tool among capable rulers, or a curse to those lacking the power to change it or having no voice in its formulation. With the law, humanity runs these risks, but without it the forces of chaos and barbarism reign supreme. We have no choice, then, but to use it while trying not to abuse it. It is a matter of balance, it seems, between two kinds of "slavery." We can be slaves to the law and lose some freedom, or be slaves to our passions and lose our dignity as authentic human beings.

We must choose very carefully, therefore, which kind of slaves we want to be. It would seem obvious that most of us do not want to be slaves of our passions, obsessed with lustful and depraved living. Under those circumstances we would be something less than fully human, our actions less dignified than the lower species, which, after all, merely follow their instincts. We must be slaves to some kind of law, then, if we hope to mature and progress to a higher level of existence, to reach our destiny as *Homo religiosus,* to fully comprehend what we already are. But if we *are* to be slaves to the law, then we should be careful as to the *kind of law* to which we bind ourselves. Religion (*religare*), as the word implies, binds us to God as our Creator and Lord. This law, especially as reduced to its simplest form, is the love of God with all the heart and the love of neighbor as oneself. Slavery to these laws is the only path that preserves and nurtures our human essence while allowing the optimum amount of freedom. This freedom, reduced to its essentials, is the freedom to love.

RELIGION AND THE LAW

The earliest legal code recovered in its entirety is the Babylonian *Code of Hammurabi*. Written in cuneiform, the ancient Mesopotamian Code dates to the eighteenth century BC, and was discovered by French archaeologists in 1901 to 1902 in Susa, Iraq (formally ancient Elam). The divine origin of the Code is emphasized in a bas-relief in which the king is depicted receiving the Code from the sun god, Shamash. The Code begins with directions for legal procedure and the statement of penalties for unjust accusations, false testimony, and injustice done by judges. Then follows laws concerning property rights, loans, debts, domestic property, and family rights. The Code of Hammurabi, unlike the *Mosaic Law*, contains no laws having to do with the worship of a deity, in spite of its purported divine origin. The basis of the law against crimes is that of equal retaliation, comparable to the Semitic law of "an eye for an eye." There are, perhaps, religious overtones to the laws that are aimed at protecting all classes of Babylonian society. These laws provided protection for the weak and the poor, including women, children, and slaves, against injustices at the hand of the more affluent.

The Hindu *Code of Manu* is another document of ancient laws, compiled in India in about AD 400. It is of interest here because of its strict laws concerning immorality. Certain offenses, such as adultery, were punished by cutting off the nose or ears. Interestingly, this practice gave rise to a rather sophisticated surgical procedure in which the nose was rebuilt from a flap of cheek or forehead skin. The integrity of the blood supply of the flap was maintained during the attachment period, or until the future nose skin had established its own blood supply. Then the flap was cut away from its original attachment site (the cheek or forehead). It was an amazing example of how a religious code can affect other aspects of society. In this case the law led to the development of a sophisticated plastic-surgery procedure, now known as rhinoplasty, far ahead of its time (Major, *A History of Medicine*, 72). Man-made laws, therefore, can directly impact scientific disciplines as well as religious practices.

Perhaps the best example of how law grew out of the pressing needs of a growing civilization is found in the *Mosaic Law* of ancient Israel. As a covenant people, the first and foremost laws—the commandments of Yahweh, the one God of Israel—were the most important:

> Then God spoke all these words: I am the LORD your God, who brought you out of the land of Egypt, out of the house

of slavery; you shall have no other gods before me. You
shall not make for yourself an idol, whether in the form of
anything that is in heaven above, or that is on the earth
beneath, or that is in the water under the earth. You shall
not bow down to them or worship them; for I the LORD
your God am a jealous God, punishing children for the
iniquity of parents, to the third and the fourth generation
of those who reject me. (Exod 20:1–5)

The Ten Commandments thus begin with what was the most
significant law of all to the Israelite people: "You shall have no gods
except me." Embodied in this law is what made the people of Israel
special, what distinguished them from their pagan neighbors, and
upon which their survival depended. All other laws were subordinate
to this one because without it they were no longer a covenant people.
Without the first commandment, they ceased to exist as a nation of
people under one God; in its absence, they could no longer be understood as the nation of Israel.

Throughout the deuteronomic histories (Joshua, Judges, 1 and 2
Samuel, 1 and 2 Kings), a form of this first commandment is repeated
over and over again. The form it takes (with some variation) is, "You
shall love God with all your heart." It was Samuel's most important
advice as he warned the people of the dangers and pitfalls of having a
king to rule over them. As David was about to die, the reins of king-
ship having already passed to his son Solomon, he exhorted the new
monarch to walk before God with all his heart. It was the most crucial advice he had to give him. Solomon, however, allowed his alien
wives (seven hundred in all, not to mention three-hundred concu-
bines) to "turn his heart" from Yahweh to strange gods. Because of
Solomon's disobedience, Yahweh promised that the kingdom of Israel
would be torn apart. By not loving God "with all the heart," so we are
told by scripture, the reign of Solomon began a downward spiral in the
history of Israel, resulting in its final defeat and exile into Babylon in
the sixth century BC.

In the smoldering remains of Israel, one could recognize little of
what had formally been a mighty nation. Israel's monarchy and the
holy city of Jerusalem, along with its Temple, constructed and then
later defiled by Solomon, had been reduced to rubble. Two of the

three pillars upon which Israel had once stood, the monarchy and the Temple, were no more. The third pillar, *the Mosaic Law*, was all that remained to the people of God. They clung to the Law, therefore, as someone about to drown in a raging flood clings to a scrap of flotsam. It was the most valuable thing to them in that foreign land of Babylonia because it represented the foundation of their existence as a distinct people of the one true God.

This great emphasis on the Law came to be the hallmark of the Jewish Pharisees. It was this overdone legalistic approach to life that Jesus, and especially the apostle Paul, objected to most vehemently. It might have served its purpose in earlier times, but it had become impotent, even a curse in some respects, in light of Jesus' message of love. (See Paul's Letter to the Galatians, often referred to, as I said, as the "Magna Carta of Christian freedom.")

Religious laws were discussed in an earlier chapter, particularly as they may be likened to a fence that surrounds something of value. The problem with such laws, if they indeed become excessive, is that the faithful may become obsessed with observing the law instead of what the law, under ideal conditions, is designed to protect. In other words, the obsession with the law becomes a matter of worshipping the fence instead of the values the fence is meant to preserve and protect. This, I believe, was the point Paul was trying to make in his Letter to the Galatians. His converts in Galatia, he feared, were making an idol of the law.

Recognizing religious law in its simplest form—*to love God with one's whole being, and to love one's neighbor as oneself*—frees us from a list of demanding do's and don'ts that serve only to frustrate our growth as authentic human beings. The do's and don'ts of the law may be necessary, as Paul believed, when one is a child, but when the person grows to adulthood, one should be able to put aside childish things. It is often said that some individuals remain children all of their lives, and the longer one remains a child into his or her adult years, the more that person fails to recognize the need for restraint and moderation in all things.

Loving God and neighbor with all the heart, therefore, is not something that allows one to escape religious law because it is the law couched in a special divine imperative. It makes sense to those who have grown beyond the dominance of youthful impetuosity. It comes naturally to those who have no need of an explanation of how it works as a true and wonderful perspective on the reality of life in this world. It is a goal and a perception of reality toward which we should all strive because, for Christians at least, it is a window to God's strategy for us. Among practical atheists, the law is the wellspring of their elevated sense of ethical conduct, even though they do not recognize its divine origins.

THE LAWS OF SCIENCE

Some distinctions should be made as to the different types of laws. One can think of laws as man-made, whether divinely inspired or not, or as the physicochemical laws of nature, which are integral to creation itself. Both kinds of law are necessary for any rational approach to existence. Human laws would be meaningless in a chaotic world without natural laws to govern what humans have no power to regulate. On the other side of the coin, the natural law would seem meaningless unless there were intelligent beings to observe it, react to its effects, and control its properties in the course of historical progress. Human beings, of course, cannot change the laws of nature, but they can direct them and shape them to support their own needs, civilized or barbaric, good or evil.

In speaking of the law, one needs to distinguish between the laws that affect science directly, and the more indirect, ethical influences. First, there are the laws of science itself, by which I mean the laws of chemistry and physics that set the limits of authentic scientific discovery. These "built-in" laws reveal themselves by the reproducibility of empirical data. That is to say, for example, two atoms of hydrogen and one of oxygen unite to form one molecule of water. The composition of water is always the same because the interaction of hydrogen and oxygen will always remain unchanged. If one were to drop a solid iron bar into a bucket of water, it would sink—today, tomorrow, next month, next year, next century, and so forth. The laws of chemistry and physics reveal to us by the reproducibility of these kinds of experiments that they are rigid and unchanging.

Scientists, therefore, have laws they can depend upon as unchanging. The investigator does not lack confidence in the laws of science, but only in how these laws might apply in complex situations. The larger the molecule—for example, one containing thousands of atoms of carbon, hydrogen, oxygen, nitrogen, as well as traces of other elements—the more difficult it is to determine how this complex chemical structure will interact with others of like or dissimilar composition. Larger molecules, such as hormones, enzymes, all kinds of proteins, lipids, and carbohydrates, have special properties that keep biochemists busy trying to understand how they work in the body. Complex molecules, like their smaller cousins, work within the same system of physicochemical laws, but learning how these molecular giants interact comes only after much painstaking experimentation.

Eventually, no matter how wonderful or elaborate the equipment for analysis, scientific discovery reaches its limits. This is true at both ends of the organizational spectrum. The vastness of the universe, its stars, solar systems, galaxies, and so on, are scientifically comprehensible only to a point. If the vastness of the universe itself is not daunting enough, scientists soon learn their limitations in attempts to explain its origins. What, indeed, *did* happen before the big bang? Some, even in the face of an impossible task, will continue seeking to advance these limits.

At the other end of the spectrum—as scientists examine the incredibly small particles that compose the material universe, the atoms themselves and their subatomic components, the awesome energy contained in the atom in terms of the Einstein equation—the limits of science apply as well. The smaller the particle is, the more sophisticated the instrument needed to explore the properties of that particle. Eventually the investigator reaches a point at which the observation itself changes the thing being observed. And science again discovers its limits, this time in the minuscule components of the universe, because at this level things become indeterminate. The uncertainty of the microworld, the world of atomic particles, matches the mysteries of the big bang origin of the universe. To be sure, it is all one gigantic mystery, regardless of the level of organization of the universe one wants to examine. The limits are always there, beckoning to us, whetting our appetites to know more, daring us to try, encouraging us to seek beyond the impossible.

As discussed earlier, it is good that human curiosity is undaunted, even in the face of impossible goals. It is natural that our curiosity has no limits, even if empirical science does. Indeed, in exploring the limits of scientific inquiry, humanity abruptly encounters the strategy of God. Our natural curiosity, especially among scientists, is never satisfied with any restrictions placed on the possible. We want to have answers for every question, discoverable by scientific methods or not. It seems that this insatiable appetite to know the unknown is basic to the human spirit, something the author of Genesis 2 elucidated in the powerful story of the Garden of Eden. It is this appetite, this curiosity to know and explain the natural world, that brings us to the brink of the supernatural.

SCIENCE AND RELIGIOUS LAW

Religion, as distinguished from science, does not have the same "internal" system of laws that govern it inviolably. Religion does, however, support the laws of science in a very special way. Science and religion share in common a trust in the laws of the universe, such that ultimately the material world has a rational basis. If religion and science did not share at least this kind of trust, this common *faith,* there would never be grounds for rapprochement between these two views of reality. Thus, as John Haught points out in his book *Religion and Science* (21), religion is supportive of science.

Beyond this common ground, science has no moral or ethical basis of its own. Libraries are full of books about scientific experiments that violate any sense of a moral or ethical code. The sad thing about this collection of books is that not all of them are fictional. Nonfiction books, too, give accounts of guinea pigs, both animals and humans alike, subjected to unimaginable cruelties in the name of *science.* Science without any moral or ethical compass is one of the most dangerous forces in the world. It is unquestionably an alarming prospect for the future of the world if science is ever allowed to move forward without some kind of ethical constraint.

Science, then, must have some sense of where to draw the line, when to stop experiments that threaten to run amuck. All the same, it is perhaps a foolish idea to expect scientists to buckle under the restraints of any religious system, nor should they. Rather, any moral or ethical influence on science, if it is to be really effective, must come directly from the religious convictions of scientists themselves, or indirectly through the legal institutions that govern the country to which the scientist owes allegiance. The direct method of persuasion, coming from the scientists themselves, seems the most desirable course. It is only human nature to reject, or at least resent, any outside controls on one's activity. Governmental proscriptions against a given scientific activity, therefore, will always provoke adverse reactions among members of the scientific community.

What is to be done, then, to protect future generations against unscrupulous experimentation? I am afraid I cannot answer that question. Perhaps someone of greater wisdom than I can see the problem more clearly and provide some answers. What I do suggest is something we should *not* do, and that is to write off those scientists who seem to have no moral foundation. Look at their criticism of religion to see if there is any grain of truth to their views. Usually there is. Good things can be used badly and often are. Human frailty and ineptitude do not disappear just because we do something in the name of religion. Karl Marx saw in religion a tendency to justify oppression on the basis of some future pie-in-the-sky reward. His solution to this oppression was, at least in the eyes of history, a wrong one, but the initial impetus for Marxism was not extinguished by its eventual failure.

Thus, it is important for the scientific community to realize, through the convictions of growing numbers of individual members, that science needs an indissoluble moral compass. Society as a whole, therefore, must never give up on the scientists who, intentionally or otherwise, ridicule our religious institutions. Antagonisms and recriminations do little but generate more of the same. The religious community would do well to consider, as a starting point for better relations, the common ground between science and religion, the shared approach to a rational universe. At that point, fruitful exchanges between science and religion can proceed at a more rapid pace. A more mature dialogue, introduced into the dialectic equation of science and religion, can only help.

Religion should always assume, looking to its own colorfully variegated past, that it will continue to make mistakes, even seem to go backward on occasion, then grow and mature, just as any child of God. Science, on the other hand, must eventually recognize its historical debt to religious enterprise, for it was the religion of ancient times that gave birth to science and provided it with the impetus to grow. Controversy itself has no doubt been a stimulus for scientific exploration. No effort fairs well in an insipid atmosphere of apathy, where there is disregard for one's failures or accomplishments. I believe the disagreements and conflicts between science and religion create the necessary ingredients for progress, both spiritually and intellectually. Therein lies the genuine value of the dialectic between these two erstwhile partners and sometimes formidable adversaries.

Universal recognition of this interdependency will probably never come in the lifetime of my generation, or of generations to come, for that matter. It is a comforting thought to me, however, that these great and seemingly conflicting forces are really in consort in the overall strategy of a powerful and yet loving God. I hope I can convey this feeling of reassurance to others because sometimes we tend to look at all the negatives in the world and become discouraged. In this case, at least, here is an apparent negative, the conflict between science and religion, that is actually a positive force in the long haul because it is part of God's plan for the human creature.

We have discussed law in this chapter, the laws of nature and of man. One might say that some of these human laws are actually laws of God, and indeed, that is an important way to look at the subject. Certainly the laws of nature are also the laws of God. Many would consider the Ten Commandments, although passed along through human agency, as inspired by God, if not the laws of God in a stricter sense. In another sense, *all* of the laws, natural and man-made alike, are within the purview of God because they are integral to God's creative plan. Christians may think they understand what this almighty plan is all about, but we are forced to rethink that conclusion in the light of the apostle Paul's words, informing us that it is beyond human comprehension, for "...no eye has seen, nor ear heard, nor the heart of man conceived, what God has prepared for those who love him" (1 Cor 2:9).

Convergence, as discussed in an earlier chapter, might be considered a force of evolution, a kind of law in its own right. This law is neither a purely natural law, nor is it a man-made law, but it subsumes both of these. The law of convergence is a suprahistorical force because it plots the direction of all creation. To some extent it can be seen as evidence of God's presence in history. In other, more striking terms, it may be considered as the primordial superego of history, a special insight given to us only if we look for it with the eyes of the heart. It is also the best evidence for creation considered as a *work in progress*, the topic to be discussed in the next chapter.

13

HUMAN CREATION AS A WORK IN PROGRESS

> My speech and my proclamation were not with plausible
> words of wisdom, but with a demonstration of the Spirit
> and of power, so that your faith might rest not on human
> wisdom but on the power of God.   —1 Cor 2:4–5

In the Introduction of this work I spoke of humankind as a work
of art, a beautiful composition that continues in each of us until the
day we die, and perhaps beyond. Indeed, we have to think of all creation as *becoming*, a work in progress, one in which our cooperation is
important. God uses the laws of physics as his brush. His paints are
the elements in every color of the rainbow, and space-time is his canvas. But his work of art is living, one which extends into unimaginable
dimensions. It is a work that allows the subject to leap from the canvas and observe what has been created, his or her own image. It is,
therefore, a composition of awesome complexity and breathtaking
beauty.

We seek to find God in the canvas and find instead our own
image. Removing the veil of the hidden God is not an easy undertaking. We seem to go in circles, seeking God, but instead learning more
about who we are. The more we learn of ourselves, the more we seek
to find the God that made us, and we always come back to the same
starting point. In returning, we find the place itself has changed
because we are no longer the same as we were when we began the
search. We are growing older…and wiser. We realize we have been
searching in the wrong places. We have been looking outside the artwork instead of inside it. Some might say we have found God, or

grown closer to finding him, with each cycle of the search. So the effort goes on, and will continue until the end of time.

THE MYTH OF THE BODY-MIND SPLIT

In the course of my career as an anatomist, I can look back upon thirty-one years of educating thousands of medical and dental students. During those years, it was my job to stress the importance of the human body in understanding the scientific basis of the students' respective professions. To this end, hundreds of human cadavers were dissected and thousands of human-tissue slides were studied in great detail. My colleagues and I taught "normal" anatomy. To understand the changes brought about by disease and injury, and most of all the pathologic conditions students would encounter in later courses, they first had to understand the normal appearances. But what is a normal cadaver? In a strict sense, these human remains would not be gracing our dissecting tables if they were normal, or had been just prior to death. It goes without saying, these former individuals had to die of something! Thus, paradoxically one might say, we used dead, probably diseased, human tissues to teach students the normal anatomical structure of living human beings.

Our humanity, or more correctly, the study of what it means to be human, is at the very core of most theologies. We seek to know God and we have a thirst for immortality precisely because we *are* human. Consciousness of our bodies and the flesh of which they are composed plays no small role in the human appetite for life after death. Without some level of consciousness of our human frailties, we would not know what it is to desire something more. Had we been crafted as immortal beings from the outset, why would we puzzle and meditate about the possibility of the experience? Thus, the very fact of our humanity, the fleshly dwelling place of the human psyche, forces us to look beyond these infirmities and to contemplate other meaningful potentialities.

Nevertheless, there is a lingering tendency to diminish the importance of the human body vis-à-vis its role in religious goals and expectations. Here, I am not speaking of some ancient heresy in which the body not only takes a back seat to religious consciousness, but also is actually construed as being evil. Such excesses, which inevitably lead to denying the fully human Jesus, are rarely encountered in modern religious thought. And yet, the persistent belief in body-soul dualism, the popular notion of "out-of-body" experiences, an excessive reaction against secular hedonism, and other such examples, lend themselves to this perception of bodily insignificance. The idea of the body as a husk, a throwaway container for the soul, seems to have gained popularity in our present age of disposable bottles, cameras, contact lenses, flashlights, and needles. This diminished emphasis on the importance of the body is certainly not a purposeful designation, or even a conscious one. Yet, one certainly hears variations of it in many spiritual circles, from guru to clergy.

These days we may hear so much about our sinful nature—our preoccupation with material wealth, gluttony, and sexual excess—that it seems quite natural to view the body from a negative perspective. Indeed, we are exposed to this negativity to such an extent that it completely blocks out, or almost so, the positive nature of humankind in the flesh. When scripture speaks of these weaknesses, it is often the natural response to think of the body as an exaggeration of its most degrading moments. Misinterpretations of the Pauline corpus in this regard tend to deny a central theme in the Apostle's theology, that is, that God's power for salvation can best be understood as working, even "made perfect," through human weakness. Paul's aphorism "When I am weak, then I am strong" (2 Cor 12:10) should not be viewed simply as a clever play on words. Rather, it reflects Paul's recognition that God's wisdom manifests itself through human weakness.

What matters here, I believe, is that human flesh is a showcase for our dependence on God's saving power, that the physical body has an important role to play in every human endeavor: from the ordinary, everyday tasks, to the most profound peregrinations of the intellect; from the trivial to the sublime.

All bodily behavior gives meaning to the world in which we live. My hands, feet, eyes, and so on, make my intentions real, make them come alive in the tangible universe. Who can ever be sure a thought or idea is real unless it is brought to light through the pen or the spoken word? Encounters with our neighbors reveal the role one's body plays in communication through speech and gesture. We become a part of one another's world through the language of the body, through

137

voice and intonation, through sign and symbol. The bodily gesture is not simply a marginal translation of a thought or an emotion. Rather, it is my anger, love, joy, happiness, and so on, in an incarnate mode of expression. To the extent that we are spiritual beings, our bodies are the incarnation of that spiritual essence, just as surely as Jesus is the incarnate God. Thus, the human body belongs to the material and spiritual orders, not as opposing forces, as some might imagine, but in a unity of purpose that may be partly subject to definition, and most certainly, partly mystery.

As I said before, to me the human body is like a symphony. One cannot look upon it as a series of notations and derive any sense of its real charm, or more particularly, its transcendent beauty. We are so used to thinking of the body as a collection of parts, and its life as an agglomeration of emotions and functions, that we lose sight of its unifying significance. It is the whole that comprises and mediates the body's beauty. It is the recognition of what it means to be authentically human, difficult as this may be, before we can even hear the symphony, much less listen intently so as to capture its beauty. Unfortunately, our world is so steeped in dualistic, body-soul, language that we cannot escape it even to relate the shortcomings of this kind of thinking. Dualism forces the body's dialogue with the world to become fragmented, so that the symphony is reduced to chaos and confusion. It becomes a cacophonous rendition of the sinful flesh.

Politicians are in the habit of describing the poor as "struggling to keep body and soul together." As an anatomist I am not so ingenuous as to believe that our flesh today will be the "flesh" of immortality. Our bodies are constantly losing cells and tissues to the process of wear and tear. As long as we live, these dying cells, or most of them, are replaced by new ones. With the exception of certain tissues (the central nervous system, for example), there is a constant turnover in the cellular makeup of the body throughout the life of the individual. This marvelous interplay of cells, tissues, and organs ends at death, and the process of tissue corruption begins. We all understand the physical consequences of death. That is why the flesh of the corpse is buried hurriedly, cremated, or embalmed for a more leisurely period of remembrance prior to burial.

And yet, while we are among the living, our senses of seeing, hearing, touching, smelling, and tasting unite bodily humankind with the world. As Francis Ryan puts it, "There is an internal coordination and collaboration of all my senses before any human consciousness thematically knows about it." One might further conclude, as does Ryan, that just as the "manifold experiences of sensate life" are united in one body, so are we also united through sensory experience with the flesh of the world (*The Body as Symbol*, 35).

The believer, while recognizing that death brings on corruption of the flesh, must also deal with the paradox of unity in the living being. Thus, faith is grounded in a milieu of rational inaccessibility, where human flesh and the divine exist together in one body. We cannot escape the mystery that surrounds this phenomenon, nor can the anatomist find it and dissect it in the human cadaver. More importantly, that is why the fleshly appearance of God's son is a central mystery of the Christian faith.

DOES THE FLESH HAVE A ROLE IN SALVATION?

What is the role of the body in relation to God's strategy for humankind? How are ideas of our humanity, and its importance to salvation, reevaluated and reinterpreted in the process of a growing religious consciousness? In this kind of study, I believe it is possible to glimpse a facet of the mystery surrounding human flesh and human frailty, as these relate to the idea of immortality.

We tend to think of ourselves as a name. I am John Shackleford, and you are Bill Hollis, or Barbara Keller, and so on. This, I believe, is a big mistake. Why? Because we are so much more than a name. What makes us who we are, then? Why are we different from everybody else, and yet so similar? I began to think of these things on the occasion of my fiftieth wedding-anniversary celebration. My wife and I stood before a crowd of about two hundred guests. Here is what I said to them:

> My good friends. You may think you know who I am after all these years, but I am afraid you do not. When I go to meet my maker and he asks me, "What is your name," I will have to tell him it is Legion. Indeed, like the Gerasene demoniac of Mark's Gospel, I am many people. You see, my

friends, I carry you with me wherever I go because you have become a part of me. Just as surely as my wife and I are united by virtue of our marriage vows, you have become a part of me through friendship. You and I are united in a special way, and not just because we are together in this room. You are a part of me because you have played a major role in defining who I am.

Thus, when my Lord asks me who I am, I will have to tell him I am many people. But unlike the Gerasene demoniac, my Lord will not cast you out into a herd of swine. You are too intimately a part of me to be cast out. I would not be me without you. To be sure, I am in you and you are in me. Sound familiar? Simply put, we are all heading down the road to becoming one. Isn't that the way it is supposed to be?

When we try to understand who God is, we end up attempting to understand ourselves. What does it mean to be human? Our view of God defines who we are, just as surely as our friends play a role in who we have become. Without friends, we would not amount to much, a blank slate, perhaps, but certainly less than an authentic human being. Looking at our humanity through our beliefs, fears, and hopes is one way to understand who we are. Thus, we are *Legion,* destined to rise above the image on the canvas to seek out what inspired such a great work of art, and to understand what it means to be children of God.

Having studied the body for the major part of my professional life, it is hard not to see in the human form a miraculous creation. I have taught in all fields of anatomy, from the gross anatomical form to the ultrastructure of the smallest cellular particle. In my research with the electron microscope, I marveled daily at the intricate composition of such tiny organelles as mitochondria, cell membranes, and endoplasmic reticulum. I know this intricacy is not a convincing argument for the existence of a personal God, but it certainly has the power to reinforce what I already believe.

Scientists speak of the statistical probabilities of life arising out of the primordial soup in the early history of Earth. Theoretical physicists write of multiple universes, perhaps parallel to our own, so numerous that one such as ours was bound to occur and to be suitable for the evolution of humankind. But once we have this marvelous coincidence of physics and chemistry, the intricacies of the human body constitute yet another statistical conundrum. How far will we go in trying to prove that we are here by accident, that, indeed, all of creation is a gigantic role of the dice?

So the existence of the human animal, capable of contemplating its own origins, is not so easily explained in the absence of a creative intelligence. To do so, the atheistic view of reality must arise from a greater depth of faith than do the theists from their position. This does not mean that we should *not* seek to explain as much as is possible by scientific investigations. I certainly do not imply that I am against any sane and morally defensible scientific endeavor. To the contrary, we should push the envelope as far as possible. Finding the limits of science is an important discovery in itself.

I believe that God created us for a reason. It is sometimes useful to "play God" and visualize how *you* would have created the world. It is a good exercise for students of theology, and not at all sacrilegious. Indeed, in playing God we come to appreciate the wisdom of God in creating us just the way he did. The big question, however, is why. Why would God want to "waste his time" on us? What is the *why* of an anthropic principle that includes the idea of design. To me, the answer is quite simple. God wants us to find him through faith, surely, but also through the eyes and ears of science as well. Once we find him in our hearts, and see what we have become or what we already are, then we love him in return for what he has done for us. Here I repeat the metaphor I used earlier: God does not want to be a tree falling in a lifeless wilderness.

I have always been fascinated by the apostle Paul's statement that in the afterlife we will be given an incorruptible "spiritual body" (1 Cor 15:42–44). This is certainly a comforting thought for someone who has spent most of his adult life in a wheelchair. And with that adult life also spent as a scientist, it occurs to me that if we are to receive a spiritual body, will it be composed of spiritual atoms and molecules? Will the spiritual nervous system be able to control its spiritual atoms, so that a person will be able to walk through walls, or eat a piece of fish, as did the resurrected Jesus (Luke 24:41–42)? It also occurs to me that we will need help in making the transition from life in a physical body to one in a spiritual dimension. Will a spiritual umbilical cord be needed?

What I believe is that we are already attached. We are all being prepared, at this moment, for the transition that will eventually come. Just as we needed an umbilical cord prior to physical birth, we also require one to help us into the next life. We may call this kind of nourishment by another name, but "spiritual umbilical cord" is a good metaphor for what is going on in our time of preparation.

For a moment, let us dwell on the real possibility that human life is a time of preparation. If such a possibility exists, it changes the meaning of existence for many of us. For one thing, death becomes a metaphor for transformation. Life itself becomes a symbol of some greater potential, as yet unrealized. Succinctly put, we are living in a state we may call the *already and not yet*. The *already* is the great gift of unrealized potential, and the *not yet* points to the future fruits of human transformation. Knowing of this possibility should change the way all of us live out our time on earth. Unfortunately, that ideal does not happen for most of us. We fail to interpret the signs of life. We place everything around us in categories, even our religious devotions. In some instances we may anthropomorphize ourselves right out of the most exciting visions of life. Unless we recognize the importance of being prepared, our view of life may be limited to an agglomeration of functions. So much time for sleeping, eating, working, playing, and more. Life *does* consist of these things, but to stop there can be deadly. Being trapped in our biological functions imprisons our minds, as well as our bodies, to the slavery of monotonous living, all because we fail to recognize the invitation to become what we are meant to be, authentic human beings.

No believer can refute the idea or the reality that we are living in a time of preparation. To be sure, by our actions, *we* may be doing much of the preparation. In a sense, by practicing what we believe, we are *creating* a "place" for ourselves in God's kingdom. One reason I think this way is because I believe in a perfectly just Creator. God knows he created us as fallible human beings, with the freedom to choose how we live our lives. In view of this kind of Creator, filled with loving-kindness for us all, he will not force us to accept his love, or to love him in return. Thus, it seems possible that if one chooses to believe in a death that leads to nothingness, *and then essentially to hope in the rightness of that belief,* it may be that such a person will be granted what he or she hopes.

On the other hand, I cannot imagine someone turning down eternal life if it is offered by a generous Lord. Perhaps, like Stephen Hawking, a person does not believe in a loving, personal God, but hopes he is wrong. In that case this person is surely to get the benefit of his doubts, as will the Stephen Hawkings and the Jean Paul Sartres of the world.

Seeing an embalmed cadaver makes one wonder, "Is life after death really possible?" Trying to imagine a dead loved one still alive in another dimension, the divine dimension of God, somehow stretches the faith to its breaking point. That is not to say that we suddenly go from believer to nonbeliever, but these faithless thoughts might cross one's mind unbidden, although some may not be willing to admit this, even to themselves.

A more difficult problem, perhaps, could surface in the case of Alzheimer's disease, or in other types of severe mental deterioration. What happens to the mind of this individual, who may not even recognize his or her own spouse? Where has the intelligence gone? The brain has deteriorated to such an extent that the person you once knew no longer lives. Your former husband or wife or friend does not exist in the body you see before you. When this husk of a person finally dies, is this pitiful remnant the essence of what will be resurrected to eternal life? What is death, after all?

Some would say, certainly the faithful Christian, that death is simply a metaphor for transformation. The fact of death, therefore, does not have the finality for the Christian that the atheist might believe to be the case. But if we don't carry our thoughts and perceptions with us to the grave, such as in Alzheimer's, where do they reside until they are reunited with the resurrected body? Does the Alzheimer's patient already have one foot in heaven, so to speak? Must one die with all his or her mental abilities intact in order to carry his full personality into the afterlife? To answer these questions I believe we must look upon the dying process a little differently than we might ordinarily.

THE DYING PROCESS

Everything we experience in life here in the material universe occupies space and exhibits three physical dimensions. In addition, science tells us there is a fourth dimension, namely, that of time. We all experience the three dimensions of our existence in terms of time—more specifically, linear time. That is to say, we go to the grocery store and buy bread. The one act (of going to the grocery store) comes before the other (buying the bread). We live and experience linear time in every waking moment and would be lost, or go out of our minds, in its absence. Everyone conceives their personal history—birth, adolescence, adulthood, old age, death—in terms of time. We may think in the same way about world history. Civilizations are born and die out, languages come and go. Wars, famine, and epidemics make headlines in one generation, while these same events fade from memory in the next. With the passage of time, current news becomes old news, and old news becomes history.

Theologians tell us that God is *timeless,* that there is no present or future for God. Is this possible? We are told that modern physics needs to accept that in some sense the future already exists (Stannard, *Evidence of Purpose,* 34). Could we humans possibly think and exist in a timeless universe if, for example, we should cross over from our universe to the divine dimension of God? How would a person so immersed in time adjust to sudden timelessness? Is it necessary that we *become like God* before such a transformation is possible? Are there other dimensions that we will one day understand when we reach a higher plane of existence? The most difficult adjustment in our new existence might be to live in the absence of time. I doubt there will be clocks in the afterlife because such trappings would be meaningless. Perhaps adjustments like this would involve some pain in the beginning. For example, I cannot even write about a timeless existence without using words that relate to time. But then, it may be that we will not be suddenly immersed in timelessness. There may be a transition.

It is natural to think of dying as an event that occurs suddenly, within seconds or minutes, especially in cases of severe trauma. But how do we know this to be true of the person actually experiencing death? Perhaps time is not measured by the same parameters. What seems to family members as the minute their loved one's heart stops beating and brain death occurs may represent an expanded period to the dying person. I do not mean to imply that suffering is prolonged. I am speaking of that interval following the apparent loss of consciousness, that is, the transition period from life to the transformation we call death.

It may even be that we die in much the same way as we gestate in our mother's womb. As I said earlier, perhaps there is even a spiritual umbilical cord that gradually introduces us to our future home in the afterlife. The more I think about it, the more sense it makes to have the comfort of a spiritual nurturing from God (the umbilicus) during the gestation of our spiritual bodies. Otherwise, the shock of going from a time-ordered existence to a timeless one would seem an almost impossible hurtle.

In this vein, perhaps the Alzheimer's patient already does have one foot in heaven. I suggest that the intelligence of a person so disposed has already entered the spiritual dimension, at least partially so, but the umbilical to the material world has not yet been severed. What we see in the realm of the living defines for us the moment of death, whereas the person dying may be already experiencing a spiritual existence beyond death.

But, you say, this wonderful transformation does not occur until the end of the world, when all will be changed as the last trumpet sounds. To this I remind you that we are imposing a time limitation on death and the afterlife. From the last stick of the needle before bypass surgery until I awakened afterwards, I felt absolutely no sense of the passage of time. It was as though less than a split second occurred, if that much, during the entire eight hours of my surgery, before I woke up in the intensive care unit. Now, there is no better anesthesia than death, at least as far as we know. In this sense, when we die, after the "physical umbilicus" has been cut, we may experience no passage of time before reawakening in a resurrected body.

One thing for sure, when we die, we leave behind a life of sin and suffering. But why did we first have to go through all those terrible experiences that most of us, at some time, must suffer through? What was the purpose of it all, and what does it mean to us in our new existence after death? Some would argue the point, but I believe the suffering of our human bodies is needed for salvation. As mysterious as it may seem, it is an integral part of God's strategy for us, which demonstrates the wisdom of the body, for the wisdom of the body is God's wisdom in creating us as vulnerable human beings. Even death and decay, considered in the same context, must also be the wisdom of God.

14

THE WISDOM OF THE BODY

As he and his disciples and a large crowd were leaving Jericho, Bartimaeus son of Timaeus, a blind beggar, was sitting by the roadside. When he heard that it was Jesus of Nazareth, he began to shout out and say, "Jesus, Son of David, have mercy on me!" Many sternly ordered him to be quiet, but he cried out even more loudly, "Son of David, have mercy on me!" Jesus stood still and said, "Call him here." And they called the blind man, saying to him, "Take heart; get up, he is calling you." So throwing off his cloak, he sprang up and came to Jesus. Then Jesus said to him, "What do you want me to do for you?" The blind man said to him, "My teacher, let me see again." Jesus said to him, "Go; your faith has made you well." Immediately he regained his sight and followed him on the way.

—Mark 10:46–52

Of all the teachers we have in this world, the body is among the best we have. Some may take issue with this assessment, saying that all the body does is to "lead us into temptation," and this would be true, up to a point. The body also helps us to develop a moral compass. From our earliest childhood we learn what it is to have pain. We witness others' sufferings and are glad when misfortune does not happen to us as well. Included among our appetites for food and water is the desire for self-preservation, even beyond our existence here on earth. Unlike school days, our bodies are lifelong teachers. Unfortunately, many of us fail to listen to them, to hear the message our bodies bring to the senses on a daily basis.

THE BODY AS A MICROCOSM

As a youngster, I could appreciate the concept of the body likened to a small world. Even though I never had anyone explain it to me, I had knowledge enough to understand the idea, probably at least as much as our ancient forebears did. As adults, we can imagine the human body as a small world with even smaller cities inside. One city communicates with other cities through the nervous system. The world has bodily extensions—the arms, legs, hands, feet, and head. On the surface of the head, there are special sensory organs, the eyes and ears. There are openings through which the world takes in nutrients and expels waste. Thus the world of the body has a means of receiving food and getting rid of food waste via a very efficient sewer system (from the mouth to the bowels and urinary tract). The world's air conditioning system brings oxygen to its members and removes toxic substances such as carbon dioxide. This special world also has its own police force, called the immune system, which guards the city residents against attack from alien invaders. The white blood cells are its front line of defense. As the body's central division, or headquarters, the brain directs the activities of the arms, legs, hands, and feet. The heavy movers of this world are the muscles of the body. These powerful machines are constantly fueled by specialized little factories that convert food nutrients to muscle energy.

An extensive system of internal communication constantly informs the headquarters of what is going on in the cities. It also reports on conditions from the outside environment. Changes in outside conditions, especially dangerous ones, may require quick action from headquarters to activate the muscular system, moving the body from one place to another. Headquarters is constantly integrating all the information from inside the cites of this world (body), as well as that coming from the outside.

But headquarters does not control everything in this bodily world. It has endocrine substations that make special devices (hormones). The citizens that manufacture the hormones take over certain duties that the headquarters requires of them. While headquarters is busy with other things, the regulation of certain bodily functions is delegated to the endocrine substations.

People of ancient times had no idea of the complexity of bodily functions as we have today. Yet they were aware of living in their own bodies, the fleshly home of life itself. Even without the sophisticated knowledge we possess, the ancients had an innate sense of the body as a small world. And through this small world of the body (the microcosm), they communicated with the larger world of society (the macrocosm). In a sense, we live in two worlds; the smaller, more intimate world of the body, and the larger, societal world made up of others like ourselves. We arrive at an assessment of who we are by how our friends and relatives of the larger world react to us. Thus, there is a continuous interaction between the two worlds, the microcosm (of the body) and the macrocosm (of society).

The blind man Bartimaeus, mentioned at the beginning of this chapter, is a good example of the interaction between the two worlds, the small world of the body and the larger societal world. A blind beggar in first-century Palestine would have been regarded as almost worthless from the point of view of work, family, and social standing. Sighted, Bartimaeus might have been a respected merchant, and possibly a rich one. He could have been almost any kind of person, perhaps regarded as a respected and prosperous member of society. But he was none of these. He was a blind person reduced to begging in the streets for his livelihood.

In the story he cries out to Jesus to heal him of his affliction. Out of his misery and apparent worthlessness he seeks out a higher power, and finds it in one who can legitimize his existence as a human being created in the image of God. In answer to Bartimaeus's plea, the power of God comes to this man *through* his human weakness, his blindness. As a rich merchant, would he have called out to God? Perhaps so, but only if the rich merchant recognized his own vulnerability and dependency on a higher power. It is unlikely, however, that anyone would have cried out with more intensity than the blind Bartimaeus.

Mark's Gospel goes on to tell us that Bartimaeus was healed of his blindness and became a follower of Jesus. He became healed of his physical affliction, which, in turn, became a key to his spiritual growth. He was also able to join the society in which he lived, where before he was denied full access because of his blindness. God's wisdom in creating us as weak and vulnerable human beings is amply illustrated in this story.

Among social scientists, it is hypothesized that a symbolic relationship exists between society and the physical body as "macrocosm to microcosm" (Neyrey, *Paul in Other Words*, 12). The body, therefore, can be viewed as a model that represents *any* bounded system, so that the manner in which the body is perceived relates to how the cosmos is perceived. A key concept that some derive from this relationship is that bodily control is somehow an expression of social control, that is, how that control—that behavior—is preceived by society. But how might all this relate to Bartimaeus and the people of the Bible?

ISRAEL—INDIVIDUALS AND SOCIETY

We should be wary of carrying our modern analogy too far, or of attributing everything done or said in the Old Testament to some kind of body and societal interplay. In other words, how can we expect to call upon some kind of Olympian immunity from our own prejudices in order to see with unclouded eyes the full significance of the Israelite experience? Having said this, however, it should be clearly evident that the people of the Bible thought and acted to a significant degree in terms of bodily reference. The Old Testament characters frequently ascribed or relegated a specified action to a bodily part; for example, the lips say this, or the eyes behold that, instead of saying I say this, or I see that. One might advance the proposition that the Israelite people, through bodily references, were immersed in their own private world, their microcosm.

This is not to say that the Israelite was even aware of him- or herself as an individual in the same sense that we think of ourselves in a modern-day setting. To be sure, it is the conclusion of Hans Walter Wolff (*Anthropology of the Old Testament*) that the life of the ancient Israelite was so firmly integrated into family and community that to be set apart or isolated was a threatening and fearful prospect. It was inconceivably painful, according to Wolff's thinking, for the Israelite to contemplate a personal separation in which he or she must subsist as an individual, alone and without recourse to any kind of collective consciousness.

During the period beginning with Jeremiah's ministry (about 627 BC), the covenant society and the individual's place in it would undergo dramatic changes. The sufferings set forth by Jeremiah, believes Gerhard von Rad (*The Message of the Prophets*), were not just the concern of the individual prophet. These were experiences common to all. Jeremiah perceived failure not only in the community but also in the individual. Yahweh is from this time forward to bypass the old way of speaking with his people and put his will directly "into Israel's heart" (see Jer 24:7, 31:33). Because of these changes the old and familiar will be modified, such that Israel is now led by way of individualization into a new kind of community. In this detachment of the individual from the suggestive power of society, the individual is confronted with the love of God directed toward him as a person. It is not the least of biblical contributions to anthropology, believes Wolff, "that man should understand himself for the first time when he is an individual, summoned through the call of the incomparable voice out of the bonds of his heritage and called to a new covenant" (*Anthropology of the Old Testament*, 222).

John Bright, in his Anchor Bible commentary on Jeremiah, looks at this change in terms of the dark days the people of Israel were facing. The preaching of Jeremiah and Ezekiel enabled the people to survive their dark future: the Babylonian exile and the destruction of Jersulem and the Temple. These prophets, without fully knowing why they did so, prepared the way for a new community of Israel, which they hoped would one day rise out of the wreckage of the old. This would be a community based upon individual decision and loyalty in a way that the old had not been. Bright goes on to explain that the old national community—as well as "national guilt"—yield to personal responsibility. Thus, if Israel were to survive the horrifying experience of the Babylonian exile and return to anything resembling its previous independence during the glorious days of the Davidic kingdom, its new existence would be a community based on the loyalty and personal commitment of individuals. Such a greatly changed community did, in fact, emerge, Bright asserts, in the Exile and after. This changed outlook was due largely to the fact that Jeremiah and Ezekiel stressed the inward and personal nature of humankind's relationship to God.

This sad and tragic time for Israel was certainly a turning point, not only in its long and tumultuous history, but in its self-image as well. It had lost almost everything. In the tragedy of the exile, the Jews found themselves far from their homes, without temple and without cult. And yet they had their "new heart," which would give them a whole new way of looking upon themselves, their religion, and the world around them. Even in the land of their exile, after the blow had fallen, it would be Jeremiah who was the first to assure them that they could meet their God—without temple and without cult—if they sought him with all their heart.

It seems impossible to overemphasize the importance of human weakness in God's strategy for human salvation. We are weak because of our physical limitations as well as our emotional ones. And yet it is through this very weakness that the wisdom of the body becomes evident. Nobody goes out looking to suffer, to be blind or deaf, or to have a crippled body. Even worse than such physical difficulties are the prospects of mental and emotional sicknesses. Thus, we pray for deliverance from these things. We ask God to help us in our most difficult moments. Moreover, the problems faced by one individual are multiplied a million times over in the larger world of society. We may be lucky enough to be blessed with a relatively healthy body, and yet, we cannot escape the suffering that surrounds us if we merely open our eyes and ears.

All of society is vulnerable to these difficulties, and together we pray and worship for deliverance. In this sense, religion begins with the recognition of our human weakness, individually and collectively. We take solace in sharing our problems with one another, and praying together for deliverance from them. Since we know that we will never escape suffering and pain in this life, we hope for a life in which our suffering will come to an end and we will live in happiness forever, for "God will wipe away every tear" (Rev 7:17). Viewed from this perspective, our suffering becomes more meaningful, our weakness becomes more bearable, and our future becomes more optimistic.

Human weakness, then, leads to religious striving, to hope in a future of things not possible in this life. How we go about this kind of struggle for understanding, for solace in our pain and helplessness, also reflects the wisdom of the body. Were we to be saddled with debilitating conditions and have no means to look beyond them, we would truly be a pitiable lot. To be given an appetite for immortality with no means to satisfy that longing, would be a cruel hoax indeed. So how do we reach out to a God so powerful as to be almost incomprehensible? It may be an impossible task. We live in a universe so vast and complex as to boggle the mind, but we reach out to this mostly incomprehensible God, nevertheless.

THE BODY AS A REFERENT TO GOD

In order to understand God from our limited human perspective we tend to view him in human terms. We do this by magnifying some human attribute in our imagination. For example, God's goodness is human goodness expanded to an infinite degree. We know no other way to think of divine goodness beyond what we experience on earth. All we can say is that God's goodness must be much better, perhaps infinitely so, than any human's goodness. The trouble may be that we humans cannot begin to understand what *infinite goodness* might be. We can only dream about it and wonder.

In our approach to the divine we also tend to impart to God certain physical attributes. In the Old Testament, God not only has a voice, but possesses such anatomical features as eyes, ears, hands, arms, and feet. Understanding God in human terms, as did the ancient Israelites, made him more approachable. Scholars refer to this literary device by the term *anthropomorphism*. This practice is found throughout the Old Testament and, to a lesser degree, in the New Testament as well. One of the most extensive examples of an anthropomorphism is the "voice of God." It is used more than twenty times in Deuteronomy alone.

Reference to the voice of God is not, as one might think, made out of ignorance of the Deity. In most cases the biblical author is not referring to an actual sound coming out of the spirit dimension that can be detected by the normal human ear. Rather, it is an abstraction that requires a special kind of hearing. The voice of God is not heard, nor listened to, by those who are "hard of heart." Anatomical integrity of the hearing mechanism is not a factor in hearing the voice of God. Furthermore, a person may "hear" God's voice even though totally deaf to ordinary sounds.

The functioning ear is important, nevertheless, in the overall scheme of salvation history. That is to say, without the functional ear, there would be no basis for the symbolic organ that hears and listens to the voice of God. The same is true for other anatomical parts. One cannot invent a meaningful symbol unless the figurative sense has some grounding in physical reality. Thus, we have used our bodies throughout history to point to a reality that transcends its human starting point.

EARS THAT HEAR THE VOICE OF GOD

Suppose you entered a dance hall and saw a large group of people dancing. There was another group milling about, apparently with no interest in participating in the dance. That was because the inactive group could not hear the music. In fact, there was a beautiful melody seeming to emanate from the rafters, but there was no musician visible, no banjo being plucked, no sweaty fiddler playing his heart out. Since there was no music coming to the ears of the inactive group, they did not, or could not, participate in the joyful celebration of the dance.

Eventually the ones who could not hear the music became infuriated with those who kept on dancing, because they could not do the same. They left the dance floor in frustration, then began to laugh and point their fingers at the group still dancing. "How stupid they are," they shouted. "Look at them out there, pretending to hear the music when there is none to be heard." The more beautifully the dancers moved, the more outlandish were the insulting cries coming from the ones standing on the sidelines.

Doesn't this sound familiar? Doesn't the above scenario make a wonderful metaphor for those who laugh and make fun of religious devotion? The critics think they know all about religion because they tried it and it didn't do anything for them. The dancers, of course, are those who hear the word of God and do it. As the prophets say, let those who have ears to hear listen to the voice of God. The case for *spiritual deafness* is a good one. We merely need to look around to see it in action, to see the skeptics, through omission or commission, making fun of those who hear the music.

It would be difficult to overestimate the importance of the faculty of hearing in spirituality, especially to the ancient Israelite. One receives wisdom and is transformed by it through the organ of hearing. The very institution of a people of God begins with hearing the

words of Yahweh. This relationship continues and is constantly rein-
forced in the lives of the people, such that, "one does not live by bread
alone, but by every word that comes from the mouth of the LORD"
(Deut 8:3).

> Give ear, O heavens, and I will speak;
>> let the earth hear the words of my mouth.
> May my teaching drop like the rain,
>> my speech condense like the dew;
> like gentle rain on grass,
>> like showers on new growth.
> For I will proclaim the name of the LORD;
>> ascribe greatness to our God!
>
> The Rock, his work is perfect,
>> and all his ways are just.
> A faithful God, without deceit,
>> just and upright is he. (Deut 32:1–4)

This beginning of the Song of Moses highlights the importance
of hearing. The Hebrew word for *hear* (*shema*) often carries the impli-
cation to attend what is heard with awareness and obedience. Not just
the present, but all the future, depends on the people hearing (and
hearing again) these words. The words will be remembered by a
people, "a people living, sinning, and struggling in the dust of history,"
says Harold Fisch (*Poetry with a Purpose*, 64). The Song of Moses,
says Fisch, echoes endlessly throughout the Psalms and the prophetic
books, its poetry and words remaining potent, in spite of the lapse of
time. The words will be laid up by the people (see Deut 32:40) to
explode within them in the midst of future need. Heaven and earth in
the Hebrew imagination are significantly different from what we may
think of as the cosmos. They belong, rather, to the broader scheme of
a contractual history. When the contract is broken, which occurs frequently in the course of history, the prophet's oracles repeatedly cry
out for Israel *to hear:*

> Hear, O heavens, and listen, O earth;
>> for the LORD has spoken:

I reared children and brought them up,
  but they have rebelled against me.
The ox knows its owner,
  and the donkey its master's crib;
but Israel does not know,
  my people do not understand. (Isa 1:2–3)

The importance and urgency of the cry to hear does not diminish in New Testament times. In the Gospel of Luke, those who hear and do the will of God become the mother and brothers of Jesus (Luke 8:21; see also Matt 12:50; Mark 3:35). Paul asks the question (Rom 10:24), "How are [people] to believe in him of whom they have never heard? And how are they to hear without a preacher?" To Paul the very foundation of faith lies in hearing the gospel of Christ.

The body is wise, indeed. It speaks to us from the day we are born until we leave this earth. As said earlier, we are a work in progress, a beautiful composition that will continue in us, perhaps even after death. We participate, along with our Creator, in bringing the artwork of the human body to fruition. From the evolutionary perspective, the human body is an even more beautiful composition, for through this magnificent process we can see the hand of God more clearly. Reflecting on our own origins, we can see the patterns and the vectors that point to an ascendancy of even greater heights. Though we cannot visualize its final beauty, we can imagine a composition worthy of the God who created us from the beginning, and this is a marvelous thought to hold.

15

SCIENCE, RELIGION, AND THE CRUCIBLE OF TIME

The kings of the earth set themselves,
    and the rulers take counsel together,
    against the LORD and his anointed, saying,
"Let us burst their bonds asunder,
    and cast their cords from us." —Ps 2:2–3

Time is the crucible in which science and ethical behavior are tested and brought to the forefront as a necessary, even indispensable, relationship. Science is neither good nor bad. It has no moral ground from which to limit its incursions into the affairs of humankind. It simply is. Science does, however, spring from the human intellect, a gift from God. Science and religious consciousness, like devoted lovers, must work together to achieve the ends for which the gift is made, or all is for naught. And nothing brings out the necessity of this relationship more than the crucible of time. It takes time for science to reach its fullest potential, whether as a boon to the survival of humankind, or sadly, as the means for its utter destruction. By the same token, the religions of the world need time to mature in outlook and to insert creative direction into the mentality of a civilization intent on destroying itself. We are our own worst enemy, and we are in dire need of a loving God to save and guide us.

The greatest danger is for one partner to outdistance the other. It will not work, for example, for science to lead the way with a core of moral restraints tagging along like a petulant backseat driver. This would surely be a prescription for disaster. Only time will tell if the partners can grow and mature together sufficiently to prevent a human cataclysm. Some areas, such as natural disasters, provide a common ground of opportunities for working together. Natural disasters make a fertile background for the ideal partnership between science and religion.

However, there then arises the difficult problem, theologically speaking, of the perceived evil in natural disasters. Hurricanes, earthquakes, and tsunamis can all be blamed on God and used as an argument against the existence of a loving God. Why would the God of Christians, Jews, and Muslims allow such violence to occur against his helpless creatures? It would be a cruel God, indeed, to *will* such disasters to occur, and we cannot blame them on human freedom as we can sinful behavior. What *can* be said about natural disasters, from a faith perspective, is that God *allows* these things to occur for a definite reason, one that may not be perfectly clear to his human creatures. All things considered, science has shown its true value when it comes to the benefits to humanity in minimizing the devastation of natural disasters.

SCIENCE AND NATURAL DISASTERS

Let us stop for a moment and look at what humanity has done in the past in response to natural disasters. For hurricanes we now have hurricane-hunter planes to pinpoint the eye of the storm, calculate its direction, and warn the population in its path. Satellite imagery also aids in tracking hurricanes, as well as allowing worldwide communications regarding events such as these. Seismographs study and predict the likelihood of earthquakes and volcanoes. In certain areas, tsunami warnings are also possible. Unfortunately, such was not the case in the 2004 tsunami in Southeast Asia, in which hundreds of thousands of unsuspecting people were killed, while millions more were made homeless.

As tragic as natural disasters can be, they also stimulate the scientific world to try and find ways of minimizing the death and injury toll. Indeed, some of our most sophisticated scientific discoveries have occurred as a result of natural disasters, along with the impetus to investigate them. The earth sciences, advances in medicine, the exploration of space, and all kinds of technical discoveries can be related in some way or another to the stimulus brought on by natural disasters.

It is through scientific discoveries that the faithful person is led to a greater understanding of creation, and thus the God who is responsible for it all. One could say, therefore, that God allows natural disasters because it is a part of his strategy for our salvation. Eventually, scientists and theologians alike should come to a greater appreciation of this evidence. Oftentimes, it is the unsuspected spin-off of an invention that turns out to be as or more valuable than the original objectives of the investigation itself. Such is certainly true of the benefits passed on to medical science as a result of the space program. Miniaturization, for example, an essential requirement of launching space craft at a minimal cost in fuel, has given medicine some of its most sophisticated instruments, which impact directly many more people than the space program. The cardiac pacemaker, which can be implanted inside the chest, is just one example of such technological "side benefits."

When natural disasters appear on the world stage, they also provide the impetus for better communication. In our need for better technology in this area, science has brought about an almost unbelievable array of advances. Satellites orbiting the planet have brought us closer together as a world community. As such, we have become more profoundly aware of the diversity among members of the human family. The horrors of human rights' abuses are much more visible than they once were. Dictators and repressive governments still get away with murder, but other nations know about them and can authorize penalties against such behavior.

Thus, advances in worldwide communications are among the greatest of scientific gifts to humankind. It has already brought the human family closer together. We are in a position to understand one another more than at any other time in our history. It is further evidence of the phenomenon of the convergence that is going on at this very moment. We are a long way from becoming a world of united values and moral outlook, but the seeds of this marvelous transformation have already been planted.

Of course, there are many other ways in which scientific curiosity is stimulated, aside from natural disasters. Other types of disasters that have an effect on science are debilitating medical pathologies, accidental injuries, and so on. These may be thought of as natural disasters because they were not the result of evil intentions. The vast majority of research efforts and grant monies in this country are devoted to discovering the causes of catastrophic illnesses. Through advances in medical science and their applications, we have come a long way in understanding the human body and its vulnerability to illnesses of all kinds. These discoveries, although providing comfort to many individuals, also serve to remind us of our mortality as human beings.

Being aware of our physical frailty is not all bad. It certainly stimulates many to think beyond their existence in the here and now, and to take the next step in contemplating the ultimate meaning of life. Are sickness, illness, and death, with some joyous moments in between, what life is all about? Should I be more aware of the deeper mysteries of life and death, and tailor my time here accordingly? These are all good questions to ask oneself because they usually help us to grow and mature as authentic human beings. Personal difficulties, including natural disasters, force us to examine more far-reaching questions.

The contributions of science in ameliorating natural disasters is perhaps more fortuitous than first meets the eye. We have seen how the spin-offs of scientific research in this area have benefited weather prediction, the practice of medicine, space exploration, and worldwide communication. In the process of cooperating in reducing the perils of natural disasters, science and religion have learned how to work together, at least in a limited sphere. This level of cooperation has not gone unnoticed on the scale of global consciousness. This may be an example of the two pursuits, of the grand partnership of science and religion growing up together. History will tell if we have grown closer to wholeness in these efforts to make it work in other areas.

SCIENCE AND THE EVILS OF WAR

Explaining the cruelties of war might not be as simple as blaming such nonsensical acts on human sinfulness. As science does something to minimize the tragic effects of natural disasters, God wants us to do something about the abuses of human freedom. It is so easy to excuse oneself from any responsibility for an act of war when it occurs in some foreign land. Out of sight, out of mind, as the saying goes. But God does not allow us to dismiss war, at any time or in any place, so easily. Here again, God is trying to teach us something, and the lesson goes beyond making sinful conduct into an excuse for human cruelty. War is the greatest symbol of human failure (See my book, *God as Symbol*). Until we realize the full implications of that reality, humanity will continue to make the same mistakes over and over.

At first glance, at least, it may seem that science has done nothing to benefit humanity in this regard. The weapons of war, which are the products of scientific research and development, only make the killing fields larger and less discriminate. The innocent die along with the combatants in increasing numbers. So is there any positive aspect of science's participation in war? Not much, it would seem. As individuals, of course, scientists can refuse to participate in building weapons of war, but there are always others who will take their place in developing these engines of evil.

In one sense, science is responsible for making war into a self-limiting process. The weapons, particularly nuclear devices, have become so awesomely destructive that their use is almost prohibitive. Certainly a global nuclear war is unthinkable because such a conflict would spell the end of human civilization, if not all living beings. Is there a strategy of God to be read into this scenario? Is the crucible of time at work in this instance?

One could attempt to look upon weapons of war from God's point of view. From this perspective, it could be said that we are being tested as to our worthiness to continue to exist as God's children. We are placed in a crucible of our own making. Through the endeavors of science, we can make our world better for all people, or we can destroy it. The choice is ours: Has our moral compass developed enough at this time in history to prevent the unthinkable?

When I was twelve, we entered World War II. It was all very exciting, even romantic, to think of going to war against the "evil" Germans and Japanese. I had no clear picture of what war was all about. The newsreels we saw at the movies spoke mostly of victories and heroism, all of which fed my naive ideas about war. My brother wrote home about his life in the army, but he was a supply sergeant and never saw or participated in an actual battle. My brother-in-law trained pilots in a Naval air base. He never saw actual combat either. All and all, the horrors of war never came to my attention until after it was over. Physically speaking, and in terms of my pubescence, I grew up during the war years. Put another way, between Pearl Harbor and the surrender of Japan aboard the Battleship Missouri, my hormones began to percolate through my young body. At that age I gave little thought to the moral implications of war. Certainly, if any war could be justified on a moral basis, it was World War II, being fought against the evils of Nazism.

The cost of World War II was staggering in terms of lost life, much less economics and property. By some estimates of both military and civilian populations, more than fifty million men, women, and children were killed. The United States was fortunate in not suffering large civilian losses as did the USSR, China, Germany, Poland, Japan, France, and Britain. Smaller countries such as Yugoslavia, Romania, Hungary, and Czechoslovakia also suffered significant losses to their civilian populations.

War is the greatest reminder of our human failings, a fault in the human character in its inability to control its most despicable attitudes and traits. No one can excuse themselves from some level of culpability. This has been our problem over the centuries—making excuses for ourselves. We cannot excuse ourselves from being human. We cannot opt out of the flow of time and the historical circumstances that place us in our present position. We are a human family, and we must take some responsibility for all the members of our family. One can, of course, blame all sinful conduct on human freedom. God gave us freedom so that we could freely love God and our neighbor as our self. Thus, we can blame the evil in the world on human free will, but that does not let us escape the responsibility to do something about these abuses.

Global communications should help us to understand more fully the nature of the human family to which we belong. We have the tools to understand other cultures and religious precepts more now than at any other time in history. Almost nothing can be done in secret anymore. As I said before, human rights' violations, in some form or another, are becoming increasingly difficult to hide. We can thank science for this simple fact. It has been used by humanity to develop weapons of mass destruction, but it has also given us the ability to monitor countries who possess them and to urge restraint in making more. The insanity of actually starting a nuclear war becomes more evident with each passing day.

Scientific curiosity is certainly a gift, freely given by the Creator, but one might ask, For what purpose? Personally, I do not believe the urges of scientific ingenuity are given to us for our comfort, even in light of its most humanitarian uses. The applications of science to heal the sick, feed the poor, and so on, though wonderful acts of mercy, are not the point I am making here. Science and all other intellectual pursuits are part of the human effort to learn who we are, and where we are going as a species. Science is one of the inescapable driving forces in the struggle for human authenticity, but only if it is perceived in the context of moral courage and righteousness. Taken together, these two forces are invincible. Divided, they will not live to bear the ultimate fruits intended for us by the gracious Lord of creation.

There are other tests waiting in the wings of the historical stage. Earlier, I alluded to the necessity of moral and ethical restraint in regards to genetic manipulation. Where do we draw the line, or better yet, how do we impose any limits whatsoever, if science and religion do not cooperate in such a perilous venture? Are we to allow unscrupulous individuals or groups free reign in their experiments on the human genome? Is there a point at which one must say no more, no more?

And then there is the problem of preserving the environment. Saving as best we can the fragile ecosystems that sustain us is as important as avoiding a nuclear war. A worldwide deterioration in the environment may kill civilization more slowly than a nuclear war, but it will kill us nevertheless. It is essential, therefore, that science and religion learn to work together in this crucial partnership. Will it happen soon enough? That is a question that only the crucible of time can answer.

SELECT BIBLIOGRAPHY

Armstrong, Karen. *A History of God*. New York: Balantine Books, 1993.

Artigas, Mariano. *The Mind of the Universe*. Philadelphia: Templeton Foundation Press, 2000.

Barrett, William and Henry D. Aiken, eds. *Philosophy in the Twentieth Century*. New York: Random House, 1962.

Beker, Christiaan J. *Suffering and Hope*. Grand Rapids: Eerdmans Pub. Co., 1994.

Birky, William C., Jr. "Transmission Genetics of Mitochondria and Chloroplasts." *Annual Review of Genetics* 12 (1978): 471–512.

Bynum, Caroline Walker. *The Resurrection of the Body*. New York: Columbia University Press, 1995.

Campbell, Joseph. *Creative Mythology: The Masks of God*. New York: Viking Penguin, 1968.

Cann, Rebecca L., Mark Stoneking, and Allan C. Wilson. "Mitochondrial DNA and Human Evolution." *Nature* 325:31–36, 1987.

Carmody, Denise Lardner. *Feminism and Christianity: A Two-Way Reflection*. Nashville: Abington, 1982.

Clift, Wallace B. *Jung and Christianity*. New York: Crossroad, 1982.

The Cloud of Unknowing. Translated and with an introduction by Clifton Wolters. New York: Penguin, 1961.

Cooke, Bernard J. *The Distancing of God*. Minneapolis: Fortress Press, 1990.

Cousar, Charles B. *A Theology of the Cross*. Minneapolis: Fortress Press, 1990.

Crews, Clyde F. *Ultimate Questions*. New York: Paulist Press, 1986.

Dudley, Donald. *The World of Tacitus*. Boston: Little, Brown and Co., 1968.

Select Bibliography

Dulles, Avery. *Apologetics and the Biblical Christ*. Paramus, NJ: Newman Press, 1971.

———. *The Craft of Theology*. New York: Crossroad Publishing Co., 1992.

Dupre, Louis. *Kierkegaard as Theologian*. New York: Sheed and Ward, 1958.

Einstein, Albert. *Out of My Later Years*. New York: Philosophical Library, 1950.

Einhorn, Stefan. *A Concealed God*. Philadelphia: Templeton Foundation Press; English trans., 2002.

Eliot, T. S. *Four Quartets*. New York: Harcourt Brace Jovanovich, 1971.

Fiorenza, Elizabeth. "Feminist Spirituality, Christian Identity and Catholic Vision." In *Womanspirit Rising*. Edited by Carol P. Christ and Judith Plaskow. San Francisco: Harper and Row, 1979.

Fitzmyer, Joseph. "Pauline Theology." In *The New Jerome Biblical Commentary*. Edited by Raymond Brown, Joseph Fitzmyer, and Roland Murphy. New Jersey: Prentice Hall, 1990.

Friedman, Maurice. *Religion and Psychology*. New York: Paragon House Publishers, 1992.

Garascia, Mary M. "Theological Anthropology." In Introduction to *Theology*. Edited by Thomas P. Rausch. Collegeville, MN: The Liturgical Press, 1993.

Garrison, Fielding H. *History of Medicine*, 4th ed. Philadelphia: W. B. Saunders Co., 1929.

Gay, Peter. *Age of Enlightenment*. New York: Time Inc., 1966.

———. *The Enlightenment: An Interpretation*. New York: Alfred A. Knopf, vol. I, 1967; vol. II, 1969.

Grant, Michael. *The Ancient Historians*. New York: Charles Scribner's Sons, 1970.

Grant, Robert. *Augustus to Constantine*. New York: Harper and Row, 1970.

Haught, John F. *Science and Religion: From Conflict to Conversion*. New York: Paulist Press, 1995.

Hawking, Stephen. *A Brief History of Time*. New York: Bantam Books, 1988.

———. *The Universe in a Nutshell*. New York: Bantam Books, 2001.

Herodotus. *The History of Herodotus.* Translated by George Rawlinson, edited by Manuel Komroff. New York: Tudor Publishing Co., 1956.

Horgan, John. *The End of Science: Facing the Limits of Knowledge in the Twilight of the Scientific Age.* Reading, MA: Helix, 1996.

Jantzen, Grace M. *Julian of Norwich.* New York: Paulist Press, 1988.

John Paul II. *Crossing the Threshold of Hope.* New York: Alfred A. Knopf, 1994.

Jung, Carl G. *Modern Man in Search of a Soul.* New York: Harcourt & Brace, 1933.

———. *Psychology and Religion.* New Haven: Yale University Press, 1938.

———. *Man and His Symbols.* New York: Dell Publishing Group, 1964.

Kaku, Michio. *Hyperspace.* New York: Doubleday, 1994.

Kelly, Geffrey B., ed. *Karl Rahner.* Minneapolis: Fortress Press, 1992.

Kelly, J. N. D. *Early Christian Doctrine,* rev. ed. Harper San Francisco, 1978.

Kiernan, Thomas P., ed. *Aristotle Dictionary.* New York: Philosophical Library, 1962.

Küng, Hans. *Theology for the Third Millennium.* Translated by Peter Heinegg. New York: Doubleday, 1988.

———. "Fundamentals of Trust." In *Foundations of Theological Study.* New York: Paulist Press, 1991.

Lewin, Roger. "The Unmasking of Mitochondrial Eve." *Science,* 238:24–26, 1987.

Lewis, C. S. *Mere Christianity.* New York: Macmillan Co., 1952.

———. *The Screwtape Letters.* New Jersey: Barbour and Co., 1961.

———. *The Silver Chair.* New York: Harper Collins, 1981.

Liderbach, Daniel. *The Numinous Universe.* New York / Mahwah, NJ: Paulist Press, 1989.

Major, Ralph H. *A History of Medicine,* vol. 1. Springfield, IL: Charles C. Thomas, 1954.

Marcel, Gabriel. "On the Ontological Mystery." In *Philosophy in the Twentieth Century,* vol. 3. Edited by William Barrett and Henry D. Aiken. New York: Random House, 1962.

Martos, Joseph. *Doors to the Sacred.* New York: Doubleday, 1982.

Matthews, Victor H. and Don C. Benjamin. *Old Testament Parallels.* New York: Paulist Press, 1991.

Mayeski, Mary Anne. "Theological Anthropology." In *Introduction to Theology.* Edited by Thomas P. Rausch. Collegeville, MN: The Liturgical Press, 1993.

Meier, John P. *The Marginal Jew.* New York: Doubleday, 1991.

Murray, John Courtney. *The Problem of God.* New Haven, CT: Yale University Press, 1964.

Nouwen, Henri J. M. *The Return of the Prodigal Son.* New York: Doubleday, 1992.

Otto, Rudolf. *The Idea of the Holy.* Translated by John W. Harvey. New York: Oxford Univ. Press, 1958.

Pagels, Elaine. *The Gnostic Gospels.* New York: Vintage Books, 1989.

Perrin, Norman. *Jesus and the Language of the Kingdom.* Philadelphia: Fortress Press, 1976.

Philo. *The Works of Philo: Complete and Unabridged.* Translated by C. D. Yonge. Peabody, MA: Hendrickson Publishers, Inc., 1993.

Pieper, Josef. *Guide to Thomas Aquinas.* Translated by Richard and Clara Winston. New York: The New American Library, 1962.

Rad, Gerhard von. *The Message of the Prophets.* Translated by D. M. G. Stalker. New York: Harper & Row Press, 1967.

Rohr, Richard and Joseph Martos. *The Wild Man's Journey.* Cincinnati: St. Anthony Messenger Press, 1992.

Rolheiser, Ronald. *The Shattered Lantern.* New York: Crossroad, 1995.

Runes, Dagobert D. *Treasury of Philosophy.* New York: Philosophical Library, 1955.

Ryan, Francis. *The Body as Symbol.* Washington/Cleveland: Corpus Books, 1970.

Schwartz, George and Philip W. Bishop, eds. *Moments of Discovery.* New York: Basic Books, Inc., 1958.

Shackleford, John. *The Biblical Heart: The Dynamic Union of Flesh and Spirit.* Factor Press, 1995.

_____. *Biblical Body Language: The Figurative Face of God.* University Press of America, 2000.

_____. *Science and Religion: Expelling the Demons from the Marriage Bed.* Factor Press, 2001.

_____. *God as Symbol: What Our Beliefs Tell Us.* University of America Press, 2004.

Shipley, Thorne. *Classics in Psychology.* New York: Philosophical Library, 1961.

Smith, Huston. *The World's Religions.* Harper San Francisco, 1991.

Stanton, William. *The Leopard's Spots.* Chicago: The University of Chicago Press, 1960.

Teilhard de Chardin, Pierre. *The Divine Milieu.* New York: Harper and Row, 1960.

_____. *The Future of Man.* New York: Harper and Row, 1964.

_____.*The Phenomenon of Man.* New York: Harper and Row, 1965.

Templeton, John M., ed. *Evidence of Purpose: Scientists Discover the Creator.* New York: Continuum, 1996.

Templeton, John M. and Robert L. Herrmann. *The God Who Would Be Known.* Philadelphia: Templeton Foundation Press, 1989.

Toynbee, Arnold J. *A Study of History.* Abridgement by D. C. Somervell. New York: Oxford University Press, 1957.

Turner, V. W. *The Forest of Symbols.* Ithaca, NY: Cornell University Press, 1967.

Wahl, Jean. *A Short History of Existentialism.* Translated by Forrest Williams and Stanley Maron. New York: Book Sales, Inc., 1949.

Wainscoat, Jim. "Out of the Garden of Eden." *Nature* 325:13, 1987.

Wolff, Hans Walter. *Anthropology of the Old Testament.* Philadelphia: Fortress Press, 1974.

Yarbro Collins, Adela. *Crisis and Catharsis: The Power of the Apocalypse.* Philadelphia: Westminster Press, 1984.